# THE ULTIMATE
# ST. LOUIS CARDINALS
# TRIVIA BOOK

A Collection of Amazing Trivia Quizzes
and Fun Facts for Die-Hard Cardinals Fans!

Ray Walker

ISBN: 978-1-953563-94-1

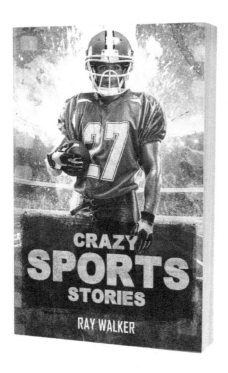

# CONTENTS

# INTRODUCTION

The St. Louis Cardinals were established in 1882 as the St. Louis Brown Stockings. After changing the name to the "Browns" and "Perfectos," the team settled on "St. Louis Cardinals" in 1900. The Cardinals have always been known as a team that fights hard and has made quite a few appearances in the MLB postseason.

This is proven by their 11 World Series championships and 19 National League pennants. They are very often a threat in the National League Central Division, having won it 11 times so far. They also have three wild card berths in franchise history (as of 2019).

The Cardinals have the second most World Championships in the MLB after the New York Yankees. They have retired the numbers of incredible players like Ozzie Smith, Stan Musial, Enos Slaughter, Ken Boyer, Dizzy Dean, Lou Brock, Bruce Sutter, Bob Gibson, Red Schoendienst, and one of the greatest MLB managers of all time, Tony La Russa. They are truly a force to be reckoned with.

The thing about baseball is that it is a lot like life. There are good times and bad times, good days and bad days, but you have to try your absolute best to never give up. The St. Louis Cardinals have proven that they refuse to give up and that they will do anything they need to do to bring a championship to the city of St. Louis. Winning is more than possible when you have a storied past as the Cards do. The Redbirds have so much captivating history and so many undeniable player legacies to be profoundly proud of.

The Cardinals are the only MLB team in the state of Missouri. Their home is Busch Stadium, which opened in 2006. The Cardinals' biggest rivals are the Chicago Cubs. With such a storied past, you're probably already very knowledgeable as the die-hard Cardinals fan that you are. Let's test that knowledge to see if you truly are the world's biggest Redbirds fan.

# CHAPTER 1:

# ORIGINS & HISTORY

## QUIZ TIME!

1. Which of the following team names was NOT a name that the Cardinals franchise once went by?

   a. St. Louis Perfectos
   b. St. Louis Browns
   c. St. Louis Perfect Stockings
   d. St. Louis Brown Stockings

2. In what year was the St. Louis Cardinals franchise established?

   a. 1892
   b. 1882
   c. 1872
   d. 1982

3. The Cardinals currently play at Busch Stadium.

   a. True
   b. False

4. Which division do the St. Louis Cardinals play in?

    a. National League East
    b. American League East
    c. National League West
    d. National League Central

5. Before 1994, what division did the St. Louis Cardinals play in?

    a. National League East
    b. American League Central
    c. American League West
    d. National League Central

6. How many National League pennants has the Cardinals franchise won (as of the end of the 2019 season)?

    a. 9
    b. 19
    c. 29
    d. 13

7. What is the name of the Cardinals' mascot?

    a. Louis
    b. Cardy
    c. Fredbird
    d. Birdie

8. Who is the longest-tenured manager in St. Louis Cardinals history (as of the end of the 2019 season)?

    a. Branch Rickey
    b. Tony La Russa

c. Eddie Dyer

d. Charles Comiskey

9. What is the St. Louis Cardinals' Triple A-Team?

   a. Lehigh Valley IronPigs

   b. Durham Bulls

   c. Charlotte Knights

   d. Memphis Red Birds

10. Who was the first manager of the Cardinals franchise?

    a. Count Campau

    b. Jack Glasscock

    c. Ned Cuthbert

    d. Ted Sullivan

11. Busch Memorial Stadium was built as a home for both MLB's St. Louis Cardinals and the NFL's St. Louis Cardinals, who now play in Arizona.

    a. True

    b. False

12. The Cardinals' current spring training home stadium is Roger Dean Stadium. Which other MLB team calls Roger Dean Stadium home during spring training?

    a. New York Mets

    b. Atlanta Braves

    c. Washington Nationals

    d. Miami Marlins

13. How many appearances has the St. Louis Cardinals franchise made in the MLB playoffs (as of the end of the 2019 season)?

a. 33

b. 29

c. 21

d. 17

14. How many World Series titles have the Cardinals won (as of the end of the 2019 season)?

a. 8

b. 9

c. 11

d. 15

15. The St. Louis Browns, Perfectos, and Brown Stockings never made it to the playoffs.

a. True

b. False

16. Which stadium was the first home stadium of the St. Louis Cardinals franchise?

a. Busch Stadium

b. Sportsman's Park

c. Busch Memorial Stadium

d. Robison Field

17. As of the end of the 2019 season, how many wild card berths have the Cardinals had in franchise history?

a. 0

b. 2

c. 3

d. 5

18. How many World Series did the St. Louis Browns win?

    a. 0
    b. 1
    c. 2
    d. 3

19. Which team is NOT currently in the National League Central Division alongside the Cardinals?

    a. Milwaukee Brewers
    b. Chicago Cubs
    c. Houston Astros
    d. Pittsburgh Pirates

20. Out of all the teams in the NL Central, the Cardinals have won the division the most times.

    a. True
    b. False

# QUIZ ANSWERS

1. C – St. Louis Perfect Stockings

2. B – 1882

3. A – True

4. D – National League Central

5. A – National League East

6. B – 19

7. C – Fredbird

8. B – Tony La Russa

9. D – Memphis Red Birds

10. C – Ned Cuthbert

11. A – True

12. D – Miami Marlins

13. B – 29

14. C – 11

15. A – True

16. B – Sportsman's Park

17. C – 3 (2001, 2011, 2012)

18. A – 0

19. C – Houston Astros (American League West)

20. A – True

# DID YOU KNOW?

1. The St. Louis Cardinals franchise has had 64 managers. They are Ned Cuthbert, Ted Sullivan, Charles Comiskey, Jimmy Williams, Tommy McCarthy, John Kerins, Chief Roseman, Count Campau, Joe Gerhardt, Jack Glasscock, Cub Stricker, Jack Crooks, George Gore, Bob Caruthers, Bill Watkins, Doggie Miller, Al Buckenberger, Chris von der Ahe, Joe Quinn, Lew Phelan, Harry Diddlebock, Arlie Latham, Roger Connor, Tommy Dowd, Hugh Nicol, Bill Hallman, Tim Hurst, Patsy Tebeau, Louie Heilbroner, Patsy Donovan, Kid Nichols, Jimmy Burke, Stanley Robison, John McCloskey, Roger Bresnahan, Miller Huggins, Jack Hendricks, Branch Rickey, Rogers Hornsby, Bob O'Farrell, Bill McKechnie, Billy Southworth, Gabby Street, Frankie Frisch, Mike González, Ray Blades, Eddie Dyer, Marty Marion, Eddie Stanky, Harry Walker, Fred Hutchinson, Stan Hack, Solly Hemus, Johnny Keane, Red Schoendienst, Vern Rapp, Jack Krol, Ken Boyer, Whitey Herzog, Joe Torre, Mike Jorgensen, Tony La Russa, Mike Matheny, and Mike Schildt.

2. Team captains for the Cardinals have been Leo Durocher (1934-1937), Terry Moore (1942-1948), and Ken Boyer (1959-1965).

3. Tony La Russa is the St. Louis Cardinals' all-time winningest manager with a record of 1,408-1,182 (.544).

4. Before they became the St. Louis Cardinals, the franchise not only did not win a World Series, they never even made the playoffs.

5. The St. Louis Cardinals hosted the MLB All-Star Games in 1940, 1957, 1966, and 2009.

6. Former MLB players/managers inducted into the National Baseball Hall of Fame as Cardinals include: Jim Bottomley, Lou Brock, Dizzy Dean, Frankie Frisch, Bob Gibson, Chick Hafey, Jesse Haines, Whitey Herzog, Rogers Hornsby, Joe Medwick, Johnny Mize, Stan Musial, Red Schoendienst, Ted Simmons, Enos Slaughter, Ozzie Smith, Billy Southworth, and Bruce Sutter. Although Tony La Russa and Branch Rickey spent most of their time with the Cards, they were not inducted as Cardinals.

7. Former Cardinals general manager Branch Rickey invented the farm system as we know it today. He was also instrumental in breaking Major League Baseball's color barrier by signing Jackie Robinson.

8. The St. Louis Brown Stockings and Browns began as a team in the American Association before they moved to the MLB.

9. The Cardinals franchise was a part of the NL East until 1994. The Cardinals won three East Division titles before they moved to the NL Central.

10. The Cardinals often boast some of the MLB's highest attendance and TV ratings.

# CHAPTER 2:

# JERSEYS & NUMBERS

## QUIZ TIME!

1. The St. Louis Perfectos' team colors were pink and purple.

   a. True
   b. False

2. Which number is NOT retired by the St. Louis Cardinals (as of the end of the 2019 season)?

   a. 1
   b. 6
   c. 16
   d. 45

3. The St. Louis Brown Stockings' colors were brown and white.

   a. True
   b. False

4. What uniform number does pitcher Adam Wainwright wear for the Cardinals?

a. 34

b. 22

c. 43

d. 50

5. What uniform number did Lou Brock wear as a member of the Cardinals?

a. 10

b. 30

c. 20

d. 9

6. Who most recently had his number retired by the Cardinals?

a. Stan Musial

b. Whitey Herzog

c. Ken Boyer

d. Tony La Russa

7. No Cardinals player has ever worn the uniform number 0.

a. True

b. False

8. Who is the only Cardinals player ever to wear number 99?

a. So Taguchi

b. Dave Wainhouse

c. Ricardo Rincon

d. Dan Haren

9. Which former Cardinals legend had his number 17 retired by the team?

a. Ken Boyer

b. Dizzy Dean

c. Enos Slaughter

d. Red Schoendienst

10. The Cardinals' logo featuring a cardinal perched on a baseball bat was first adopted back in 1922.

a. True

b. False

11. What are the St. Louis Cardinals' official team colors?

a. Cardinal red, baby blue, and sunshine yellow

b. Perfecto brown, scarlet red, blue, yellow, and white

c. Cardinal red, midnight navy blue, yellow, and white

d. Scarlet red, midnight navy blue, yellow, and white

12. Who was the first Cardinal to have his uniform number retired by the team?

a. Stan Musial

b. Ozzie Smith

c. Bruce Sutter

d. August A. Busch

13. From 1921 to 1922, the Cardinals debuted a font so large that the C would be under one armpit, while the S was under the other armpit. This made it look like each of the players' jerseys said "ARDINAL."

a. True

b. False

14. What jersey number did Jim Edmonds wear as a Cardinal?

a. 50

b. 5

c. 25

d. 15

15. What jersey number did Mark McGwire wear as a Cardinal?

    a. 50

    b. 5

    c. 25

    d. 15

16. What jersey number does Yadier Molina currently wear for the Cardinals?

    a. 41

    b. 14

    c. 44

    d. 4

17. Pitcher Bob Gibson wore three different uniform numbers over his 17 seasons with the Cardinals. Which of the numbers below did he NOT wear?

    a. 12

    b. 31

    c. 45

    d. 58

18. What jersey number did David Eckstein wear as a Cardinal?

    a. 3

    b. 11

c. 22

d. 4

19. What jersey number did pitcher Mark Mulder wear as a Cardinal?

    a. 20

    b. 30

    c. 10

    d. 40

20. What jersey number did pitcher Jason Isringhausen wear as a Cardinal?

    a. 45

    b. 48

    c. 44

    d. 55

# QUIZ ANSWERS

1. B – False

2. C – 16

3. A – True

4. D – 50

5. C – 20

6. D – Tony La Russa (2012)

7. B – False, Kerry Robinson wore it in 2002-03.

8. A – So Taguchi (He wore it from 2002 to 2007.)

9. B – Dizzy Dean

10. A – True

11. C – Cardinal red, midnight navy blue, yellow, and white

12. A – Stan Musial (It was retired in 1963.)

13. A – True

14. D – 15

15. C – 25

16. D – 4

17. A – 12

18. C – 22

19. B – 30

20. C – 44

# DID YOU KNOW?

1. The current Cardinals logo has S, T, and L interlocked. Back in 1901, the logo only had an S and an L with no T.

2. The Cardinals have retired Ozzie Smith's number 1, Red Schoendienst's number 2, Stan Musial's number 6, Enos Slaughter's number 9, Tony La Russa's number 10, Ken Boyer's number 14, Dizzy Dean's number 17, Lou Brock's number 20, Whitey Herzog's number 24, Bruce Sutter's number 42, Bob Gibson's number 45, owner August A. Busch under number 85, as well as Rogers Hornsby and broadcaster Jack Buck.

3. Two players have worn the number 00 in Cardinals history: Bobby Bonds and Omar Olivares.

4. The Cardinals debuted baby blue jerseys in 1887.

5. Before catcher Yadier Molina wore number 4 for the Cardinals, he wore number 41.

6. In 1975, the Cardinals debuted a slugging bird helmet decal. It was retired by the following season.

7. The Cardinals' mascot, Fredbird, wears a classic white Cardinals jersey with the cardinals on a baseball bat logo, as well as an interlocking "STL" hat.

8. Albert Pujols wore uniform number 5 for all of his 11 seasons in St. Louis. He still wears number 5 today as a member of the Los Angeles Angels of Anaheim.

9. Pitcher Chris Carpenter wore number 29 during all of his nine seasons with the Cardinals.

10. During the 2013 season, the Cardinals wore a Stan Musial patch on their left sleeve, because it is closest to the heart. They wore the patch to honor Musial, who passed away that year at the age of 92.

# CHAPTER 3:

# FAMOUS QUOTES

## QUIZ TIME!

1. Which famous Cardinal once said, "The first principle of contract negotiations is don't remind them of what you did in the past—tell them what you're going to do in the future."?

   a. Ozzie Smith
   b. Lou Brock
   c. Stan Musial
   d. Mark McGwire

2. Which former Cardinals player said, "I sincerely believe that there is nothing truly great in any man or woman except their character, their willingness to move beyond the realm of self and into a greater realm of selflessness. Giving back is the ultimate talent in life. That is the greatest trophy on my mantel."?

   a. Ozzie Smith
   b. Lou Brock

c. Stan Musial

d. Mark McGwire

3. Which former Cardinals manager is quoted as saying, "Pressure comes when someone calls on you to perform a task for which you are unprepared."?

   a. Eddie Dyer

   b. Joe Torre

   c. Mike Matheny

   d. Tony La Russa

4. Which former Cardinal once said, "Achieving something at home is great because I am a St. Louis Cardinal."?

   a. Jon Jay

   b. David Freese

   c. David Eckstein

   d. Michael Wacha

5. Which former Cardinals player is quoted as saying, "Show me a guy who's afraid to look bad and I'll show you a guy you can beat every time."?

   a. Ozzie Smith

   b. Curt Flood

   c. Lou Brock

   d. Red Schoendienst

6. Which former Cardinal is quoted as saying, "Having the attitude of just playing the game isn't my strength. I have to be productive. That's my responsibility."?

   a. Chris Carpenter

   b. Albert Pujols

c. David Eckstein

d. Jim Edmonds

7. Which former Cardinal is quoted as saying, "It doesn't matter the numbers, it doesn't matter the records, it doesn't matter the money that you make. What matters is to raise that trophy and to be able to bring that smile to the City of St. Louis."?

a. Jim Edmonds

b. Yadier Molina

c. Albert Pujols

d. David Freese

8. Former Cardinals pitcher Bruce Sutter once said, "A life is not important except in the impact it has on other lives."

a. True

b. False

9. Which Cardinals manager is quoted as saying, "The game has never seen a better catcher than Yadier Molina."?

a. Red Schoendienst

b. Tony La Russa

c. Mike Schildt

d. Mike Matheny

10. Which Cardinals catcher is quoted as saying, "I feel good catching and that's what I want... to feel good when I make a swing but catching is the important thing."?

a. Yadier Molina

b. Mike Matheny

c. Tony Peña

d. Tom Pagnozzi

11. Which former Oakland A's star once said, "Lou Brock was a great base stealer but today I am the greatest."?

    a. Jose Canseco

    b. Rickey Henderson

    c. Bert Campaneris

    d. Reggie Jackson

12. Which former Cardinal is quoted as saying, "I'd be lying if I told you that as a black man in baseball I hadn't gone through worse times than my teammates."?

    a. Curt Flood

    b. Lou Brock

    c. Ozzie Smith

    d. Bob Gibson

13. Which famous MLB manager once said, "The only people I ever felt intimidated by in my whole life were Bob Gibson and my daddy."?

    a. Bobby Valentine

    b. Joe Torre

    c. Buck Showalter

    d. Dusty Baker

14. Which former Cardinals manager once said, "People ask me what I do in the winter when there's no baseball. I'll tell you what I do. I stare out the window and wait for spring."?

a. Rogers Hornsby

b. Eddie Dyer

c. Eddie Stanky

d. Johnny Keane

15. Which former Cardinals player is quoted as saying, "You always believed that as good as you were, there was always somebody who could take your place. I tried to work as hard as I could to make sure that didn't happen."?

a. Dizzy Dean

b. Red Schoendienst

c. Stan Musial

d. Ozzie Smith

16. Cardinals second baseman Kolten Wong once said, "Never allow the fear of striking out keep you from playing the game."

a. True

b. False

17. Stan Musial is quoted as saying, "Back in my day, we didn't think about _____ as much. We enjoyed playing the game. We loved baseball. I didn't think about anybody else but the Cardinals."

a. Losing

b. Winning

c. Statistics

d. Money

18. Which former Cardinals player once said, "St. Louis is still going to be a special place for me, whether I'm playing 3,000 miles away or 5,000 miles away."?

    a. Mark McGwire
    b. David Freese
    c. Albert Pujols
    d. Jim Edmonds

19. Which former Cardinals player once said, "Don't turn the channel, no matter what the score is."?

    a. Scott Rolen
    b. David Eckstein
    c. Jim Edmonds
    d. Mark McGwire

20. Former Cardinal Scott Rolen once said, "I enjoy coming to the ballpark every day. I don't go to work. I come here to play."

    a. True
    b. False

# QUIZ ANSWERS

1. C – Stan Musial

2. A – Ozzie Smith

3. D – Tony La Russa

4. B – David Freese

5. C – Lou Brock

6. D – Jim Edmonds

7. C – Albert Pujols

8. B – False, Jackie Robinson said it.

9. B – Tony La Russa

10. A – Yadier Molina

11. B – Rickey Henderson

12. A – Curt Flood

13. D – Dusty Baker

14. A – Rogers Hornsby

15. B – Red Schoendienst

16. B – False, Babe Ruth said it.

17. D – Money

18. C – Albert Pujols

19. B – David Eckstein

20. A – True

# DID YOU KNOW?

1. "Performance-enhancing drugs are an illusion. I wish I had never gotten involved with steroids. It was wrong. It was stupid." – Mark McGwire

2. "I'm a lifetime St. Louis Cardinals fan." – BRAVO TV host Andy Cohen

3. "When you first hear about this guy (Stan Musial) you say, 'It can't be true.' When you first meet him you say, 'It must be an act.' But as you watch him and watch him and see how he performs and how he comports himself you say, 'He's truly one of a kind.' There will never be another like him." – Jack Buck

4. "I consciously memorized the speed at which every pitcher in the league threw his fastball, curve, and slider; then, I'd pick up the speed of the ball in the first thirty feet of its flight and knew how it would move once it had crossed the plate." – Stan Musial

5. "When I'm in my groove, there is no thinking. Everything just happens." – Ozzie Smith

6. "One year I hit .291 and had to take a salary cut. If you hit .291 today, you'd own the franchise." – Enos Slaughter

7. "Then we go to St. Louis, and you've got that tradition, that history, so spectacular. You had Hall of Famers walking around like Red and Stan in the '40s and '50s,

and you go to the '60s and you have Bob and Lou, and later in the '80s you've got Ozzie, you've got Whitey, you've got Sutter, and you feel this obligation to go forward. And from Day One, I think with the ownership we had there, we were really motivated to be caretakers, same situation, wonderful leadership, a complete package of trying to put players in a position to win. And a player that I know will be here very soon or hopefully not very soon, but some time, **Albert Pujols**." – Tony La Russa at his National Baseball Hall of Fame Induction Ceremony in 2014

8.  "Ever since I came to Cooperstown back in 1942 with the St. Louis Cardinals I've been very, very impressed by this lovely setting in Cooperstown for Baseball's Hall of Fame. And at that time, it was a thrill for me to meet Connie Mack for the first time here. And I really didn't dream, honestly, that I'd ever be back at that time, proudly to be inducted in Baseball's Hall of Fame. For even if you're confident, and I always felt I could play the game, it's presumptuous until you put together many, many good seasons to consider that one day you might have this fine day.

    "This is the greatest honor of the many that have been bestowed upon me. And it's an honor to be listed with all those great stars of yesterday and living Hall of Famers which some of them are here today. Men that I've admired as players and many who have become my good friends through the years. Fellows like Pie Traynor, Casey

Stengel, Joe Cronin, Joe Medwick, and Dizzy Dean. All of them very close to me through the years. And of course, it's an honor, too, to be inducted in the Hall of Fame with Roy Campanella, Waite Hoyt, and Stan Coveleski.

"I have no hesitation to say that St. Louis is a great place in which to live and work. We love St. Louis. And the fans in St. Louis are great. But I do hesitate to name my old teammates because we might be here most of the evening. But how could I for 22 seasons keep saying anything about a fellow who I roomed with? My old roomie, Red Schoendienst, who's a heck of a fine ballplayer and a good manager. Of course, it was great fun playing and working with Red. We had our fun as roommates and we both liked good food and legitimate shows and Red made it easy because he always made us relax. Never worried about problems so I have great affection for Red and I hope Mary, his wife, is not too disturbed by that because I really love the guy and Mary is with Red here with us today, Mary." – Stan Musial at his National Baseball Hall of Fame Ceremony in 1969

9.  "(Bob) Gibson pitches as though he's double-parked." – Vin Scully

10. "Ozzie Smith is not a uniquely talented person. In fact, he is no different than any man, woman, boy, or girl in this audience today. Ozzie Smith was a boy who decided to look within. A boy who discovered that absolutely nothing is good enough if it can be made better... a boy

who discovered an old-fashioned formula that would take him beyond the rainbow." – Ozzie Smith at his National Baseball Hall of Fame Ceremony in 2002

# CHAPTER 4:

# CATCHY NICKNAMES

## QUIZ TIME!

1. Which nickname below did Bob Gibson NOT go by during his career with the Cardinals?

   a. Gibby

   b. Hoot

   c. Gibbster

   d. Bullet

2. Lou Brock went by the nickname "The Franchise."

   a. True

   b. False

3. What is pitcher Adam Wainwright's nickname?

   a. Uncle Adam

   b. Uncle Charlie

   c. Uncle Waino

   d. Uncle Jack

4. "Albert" is a nickname. What is Albert Pujols's full name?

a. Ricardo Alberto Pujols Alcántara

b. Ricardo Alberto Pujols

c. José Alberto Pujols

d. José Alberto Pujols Alcántara

5. Which is NOT a nickname for the Cardinals as a team?

a. The Redbirds

b. Cards

c. Rally Birds

d. Birdie Boys

6. "Whitey" is a nickname. What is former Cardinals manager Herzog's full name?

a. Lorrel Elvert Norman Herzog

b. Lorrel Norman Elvert Herzog

c. Dorrel Norman Elvert Herzog

d. Dorrel Elvert Norman Herzog

7. Jay "Dizzy" Dean got his nickname from a fellow officer when he was in the military.

a. True

b. False

8. Which nickname did former Cardinals right fielder Enos Slaughter go by?

a. Poppy

b. Southern

c. Country

d. American

9. What nickname did former Cardinals left fielder Joe Medwick go by?

   a. Birdy
   b. Ducky
   c. Doggy
   d. Catty

10. What were the 1934 Cardinals referred to as?

   a. The Depression Cards
   b. The Gashouse Gang
   c. The Gashouse Cardinals
   d. The Depression Gang

11. What was former Cardinal Johnny L.R. Martin's nickname?

   a. Garlic
   b. Paprika
   c. Salt
   d. Pepper

12. Cardinals legend Stan Musial liked to refer to himself as "Stanley."

   a. True
   b. False

13. Dizzy Dean's brother Paul went by what nickname?

   a. Dilly
   b. Diffy
   c. Daffy
   d. Dally

14. Former Cardinal George Toporcer was the first non-pitcher to wear glasses on the field. What was his nickname?

    a. Specs
    b. Four Eyes
    c. Glasses George
    d. Four Eyed Topo

15. Many people liked to call former Cardinal Lou Brock the "Base Burglar."

    a. True
    b. False

16. Former Cardinal George Hendrick was known for being quiet with the media, which garnered him the nickname
    _____.

    a. Talkative
    b. Reserved
    c. Quiet
    d. Silent

17. Former Cardinals pitcher Michael Wacha goes by the nickname "Fozzie" due to the bear's common phrase "Waka Waka."

    a. True
    b. False

18. What was former Cardinal Joseph Crespi's nickname?

    a. Ghostly
    b. Crawly
    c. Creepy
    d. Wickedly

19. During 2019's MLB Players' Weekend, what nickname did former Cardinals pitcher Michael Wacha have displayed on the back of his jersey?

    a. Mike
    b. Fozzie
    c. Wachamole
    d. Wach Out

20. Jordan Hicks suffers from Type 1 diabetes. What did he have displayed on the back of his jersey during Players' Weekend in 2019 to bring awareness to the illness?

    a. Diabetic
    b. Type 1
    c. Diabetes
    d. Blood Sugar

# QUIZ ANSWERS

1. C – Gibbster

2. A – True

3. B – Uncle Charlie

4. D – José Alberto Pujols Alcántara

5. D – Birdie Boys

6. C – Dorrel Norman Elvert Herzog

7. A – True

8. C – Country

9. B – Ducky

10. B – The Gashouse Gang

11. D – Pepper

12. A – True

13. C – Daffy

14. A – Specs

15. A – True

16. D – Silent

17. B – False

18. C – Creepy

19. C – Wachamole

20. B – Type 1

# DID YOU KNOW?

1. Former Cardinal José Martinez's nickname is "Cafecito," which is the name for delicious Cuban coffee. His whole family goes by nicknames that have to do with coffee beverages.

2. During Players' Weekend in 2018, Harrison Bader went by the nickname "TOTS" because his high school friends used to call him that due to the fact that "Bader" rhymes with "tater."

3. In 2019, Andrew Miller went by the nickname "Miller Time" on his Players' Weekend jersey.

4. Cardinals legend Rogers Hornsby went by the nickname "The Rajah."

5. Stan "The Man" Musial needs no further explanation.

6. Former Cardinal Arnold McBride went by the nickname "Bake."

7. Former Cardinal James Anthony Collins went by the nickname "Ripper." As long as his first name was James and not "Jack," we're all good.

8. Ozzie "The Wizard of Oz" Smith. Again, this needs no further explanation.

9. Former Cardinals player/manager Frankie Frisch went by the nickname "Fordham Flash" and later on in his life was known as "Old Flash."

10. Yadier "Yadi" Molina. For the third and final time... this needs no further explanation.

# CHAPTER 5:

# STAN THE MAN

## QUIZ TIME!

1. What is Stan Musial's full name?

   a. Stanley Joseph Musial Jr.

   b. Stanley Frank Musial

   c. Stanley Louis Musial

   d. Stanley James Musial III

2. Stan Musial played his entire 22-season MLB career with the St. Louis Cardinals.

   a. True

   b. False

3. Where was Stan Musial born?

   a. Creve Coeur, Missouri

   b. Ladue, Missouri

   c. Shamokin, Pennsylvania

   d. Donora, Pennsylvania

4. When was Stan Musial born?

    a. June 4, 1920
    b. November 8, 1920
    c. November 21, 1920
    d. June 25, 1920

5. Stan Musial served as the Cardinals' general manager in 1967. The Cardinals also won the World Series that year.

    a. True
    b. False

6. Stan Musial was presented with the Presidential Medal of Freedom by which former U.S. president?

    a. Barack Obama
    b. George W. Bush
    c. Gerald Ford
    d. Ronald Reagan

7. How many MLB All-Star Games was Stan Musial named to during his career?

    a. 12
    b. 18
    c. 22
    d. 24

8. Stan Musial did not play for the Cardinals in 1945 due to military service in the Navy.

    a. True
    b. False

9. From 1964 to 1967, Stan Musial served as President
_____'s physical fitness advisor. His job was to
encourage physical exercise and health in Americans.

   a. Dwight Eisenhower

   b. John F. Kennedy

   c. Lyndon B. Johnson

   d. Richard Nixon

10. What uniform number did Stan Musial wear for the Cardinals?

   a. 2

   b. 3

   c. 5

   d. 6

11. How old was Stan Musial when he passed away in 2013 from natural causes?

   a. 81

   b. 89

   c. 92

   d. 99

12. Stan Musial was NEVER ejected from an MLB game in his 22-season career.

   a. True

   b. False

13. What year was Stan Musial inducted into the National Baseball Hall of Fame?

   a. 1965

   b. 1969

c. 1972

d. 1980

14. Stan Musial NEVER won a World Series with the Cardinals.

   a. True

   b. False

15. How many times did Stan Musial win the National League batting title?

   a. 1 time

   b. 3 times

   c. 7 times

   d. 8 times

16. How many times was Stan Musial named the National League MVP?

   a. 2 times

   b. 3 times

   c. 5 times

   d. 0 times

17. Stan Musial was the first player in Major League Baseball to play over 1,000 games at two different positions.

   a. True

   b. False

18. Stan Musial shares the MLB record for most All-Star Game appearances with which two former MLB players?

   a. Willie Mays and Babe Ruth

   b. Hank Aaron and Rickey Henderson

c.  Hank Aaron and Willie Mays

d.  Willie Mays and Ted Williams

19. Stan Musial also played basketball. Even though he signed with the Cardinals instead, he was offered an athletic scholarship from _____.

a.  The University of Florida

b.  Duke University

c.  The University of Kentucky

d.  The University of Pittsburgh

20. Stan Musial played on the same high school baseball team as Buddy Griffey, dad of Ken Griffey Sr. and grandfather of Ken Griffey Jr.

a.  True

b.  False

# QUIZ ANSWERS

1. B – Stanley Frank Musial

2. A – True

3. D – Donora, Pennsylvania

4. C – November 21, 1920

5. A – True

6. A – Barack Obama

7. D – 24

8. A – True

9. C – Lyndon B. Johnson

10. D – 6

11. C – 92

12. A – True

13. B – 1969

14. B – False, He won three World Series with the Cardinals (1942, 1944, 1946).

15. C – 7 times (He won in 1943, 1946, 1948, 1950, 1951, 1952, and 1957.)

16. B – 3 times (He was named NL MVP in 1943, 1946, and 1948.)

17. A – True

18. C – Hank Aaron and Willie Mays

19. D – The University of Pittsburgh

20. A – True

# DID YOU KNOW?

1. In 2007, Stan Musial was awarded the Navy Memorial's Lone Sailor Award, which is presented to Navy veterans who have led extraordinary civilian lives.

2. Stan Musial threw out the first pitch at Game 5 of the 2006 World Series. The Cardinals ended up winning that World Series. Musial also delivered the first pitch ball to President Barack Obama at the 2009 MLB All-Star Game.

3. The Cardinals have a Stan Musial statue outside of Busch Stadium. Engraved is a quote from former MLB Commissioner Ford C. Frick, "Here stands baseball's perfect warrior. Here stands baseball's perfect knight."

4. Musial was a firm believer in racial equality. He fully supported Jackie Robinson's right to play in the MLB. He also refused to endorse tobacco products once he learned that they are detrimental to your health.

5. The first sport Musial played was not baseball; it was gymnastics. His tumbling experience helped him to be more agile on the baseball diamond.

6. When Stan Musial was serving in the Navy in Hawaii, he played in an eight-team baseball league with his fellow sailors.

7. Stan Musial did not begin playing first base until 1946. Before then, he was primarily an outfielder. New Cardinals manager Eddie Dyer made the change.

8. Albert Pujols refused to go by his nickname "El Hombre" because it means "The Man" in Spanish. He believed that title should be for Stan Musial and Stan Musial only.

9. Stan Musial was the first player in MLB history to hit five home runs in a doubleheader. The only other player to do this in MLB history was Nate Colbert, who, oddly enough, was in attendance as a young boy when Musial set the record.

10. At 41 years old in 1962, Stan Musial became the oldest player in MLB history to hit three home runs in one game.

# CHAPTER 6:

# STATISTICALLY SPEAKING

## QUIZ TIME!

1. Stan Musial holds the St. Louis Cardinals franchise record for the most home runs. How many did he hit?

   a. 400
   b. 475
   c. 445
   d. 501

2. Pitcher Bob Gibson has the most wins in St. Louis Cardinals franchise history, with 251.

   a. True
   b. False

3. How many appearances have the Cardinals made in the playoffs?

   a. 24
   b. 19
   c. 12
   d. 29

4. Which former Cardinals batter holds the single-season record for strikeouts with 167 in 2000?

   a. Paul Goldschmidt
   b. Mark McGwire
   c. Jim Edmonds
   d. Ray Lankford

5. Which pitcher has the most strikeouts in Cardinals franchise history with a whopping 3,117?

   a. Adam Wainwright
   b. Lance Lynn
   c. Dizzy Dean
   d. Bob Gibson

6. _____ has the most stolen bases in Cardinals franchise history, with 888.

   a. Ozzie Smith
   b. Lou Brock
   c. Charlie Comiskey
   d. Vince Coleman

7. Jason Isringhausen holds the record for most saves in Cardinals history, with 217.

   a. True
   b. False

8. Who is the Cardinals' all-time winningest manager?

   a. Charles Comiskey
   b. Mike Matheny
   c. Branch Rickey
   d. Tony La Russa

9. Which player holds the Cardinals franchise record for home runs in a single season, with 70?

    a. Albert Pujols
    b. Jim Edmonds
    c. Mark McGwire
    d. Stan Musial

10. Who holds the single-season Cardinals record for hits, with 250?

    a. Rogers Hornsby
    b. Stan Musial
    c. Joe Medwick
    d. Jim Bottomley

11. Who holds the single-season Cardinals record for double plays grounded into?

    a. Yadier Molina
    b. Matt Holliday
    c. David Freese
    d. Albert Pujols

12. Ozzie Smith holds the record for the most sacrifice flies in all-time franchise history.

    a. True
    b. False

13. Who threw the most wild pitches in Cardinals franchise history, with 111?

    a. Bob Gibson
    b. Jesse Haines

c. Silver King

d. Jumbo McGinnis

14. Who holds the Cardinals' single-season record for most triples, with 29?

a. Stan Musial

b. Perry Werden

c. Roger Connor

d. Tom Long

15. Which hitter has the most walks in Cardinals franchise history, with 1,599?

a. Stan Musial

b. Albert Pujols

c. Ozzie Smith

d. Enos Slaughter

16. Which Cardinals hitter holds the all-time franchise record for strikeouts, with 1,469?

a. Matt Carpenter

b. Julian Javier

c. Lou Brock

d. Ray Lankford

17. Stan Musial has the most hits, singles, doubles, and triples in Cardinals franchise history.

a. True

b. False

18. Stan Musial has the most plate appearances in Cardinals franchise history, with _____.

a. 10,721

b. 12,721

c. 11,721

d. 13,721

19. Which pitcher holds the Cardinals franchise record for most saves in a single season, with 48?

a. Jason Isringhausen

b. Lee Smith

c. Ryan Franklin

d. Trevor Rosenthal

20. Bob Gibson has the most wins, losses, strikeouts, complete games, and shutouts in Cardinals franchise history.

a. True

b. False

# QUIZ ANSWERS

1. B – 475

2. A – True

3. D – 29

4. C – Jim Edmonds

5. D – Bob Gibson

6. B – Lou Brock

7. A – True

8. D – Tony La Russa (1,408-1,182 for a .544 W-L%)

9. C – Mark McGwire

10. A – Rogers Hornsby

11. B – Matt Holliday (2013)

12. B – False, Yadier Molina holds that record at 70.

13. D – Jumbo McGinnis

14. B – Perry Werden

15. A – Stan Musial

16. C – Lou Brock

17. A – True

18. B – 12,721

19. D – Trevor Rosenthal (2015)

20. A – True

# DID YOU KNOW?

1. Bob Gibson threw the most innings in Cardinals franchise history, with 3,884.1. Coming in second is Jesse Haines, who threw 3,203.2 innings.

2. Jesse Burkett has the best career batting average in Cardinals franchise history at .378. Rogers Hornsby comes in the second spot with a career batting average of .359.

3. Vince Coleman holds the Cardinals franchise record for stolen base percentage, with 82.68. Lou Brock holds the Cardinals franchise record for stolen bases, with 888. Lou Brock also holds the Cardinals franchise record for number of times caught stealing at 285.

4. Stan Musial has the most extra-base hits in Cardinals franchise history, with 1,377. Second on the list is Albert Pujols with 915.

5. Mark McGwire holds the Cardinals franchise record for at-bats per home run, with 7.9. Essentially, what this means is that during his time with St. Louis, Mac hit a home run about every eight at-bats.

6. Tyler Greene holds the Cardinals single-season record for stolen base percentage at 100! During the season, he stole 11 bases and was never thrown out. Incredible!

7. Steve Evans holds the single-season Cardinals record for the most hit by pitches with 31 in 1910.

8. Catcher Yadier Molina has grounded into the most double plays in Cardinals history, with 254 (as of the 2019 season).

9. Silver King holds the Cardinals single-season record for wins with 45 in 1888. Second on the list is Dave Foutz with 41 in 1886.

10. Red Donahue holds the Cardinals' single-season record for most losses with 35 in 1897. Bob Gibson has the most losses in Cardinals franchise history, with 174. (He also holds the record for wins, though.)

# CHAPTER 7:

# THE TRADE MARKET

## QUIZ TIME!

1. On June 15, 1964, the St. Louis Cardinals traded right-hand pitcher Ernie Broglio, outfielder Doug Clemens, and left-hand pitcher Bobby Shantz to the Chicago Cubs in exchange for outfielder _____, left-hand pitcher Jack Spring, and right-hand pitcher Paul Toth.

   a. Curt Flood
   b. Mike Shannon
   c. Lou Brock
   d. Carl Warwick

2. On December 10, 1981, the St. Louis Cardinals traded outfielder Sixto Lezcano, shortstop Garry Templeton, and right-hand pitcher Luis DeLeón to the San Diego Padres in exchange for shortstop _____, right-hand pitcher Steve Mura, and left-hand pitcher Al Olmsted.

   a. Mike Ramsey
   b. Ozzie Smith

c. Steve Braun

d. Garry Templeton

3. In 1949, Stan Musial was traded to the Philadelphia Athletics.

a. True

b. False

4. On December 13, 2003, the St. Louis Cardinals traded outfielder J.D. Drew and catcher/outfielder Eli Marrero to the _____ in exchange for right-hand pitcher Adam Wainwright, left-hand pitcher Ray King, and right-hand pitcher Jason Marquis.

a. Kansas City Royals

b. Baltimore Orioles

c. Atlanta Braves

d. Los Angeles Dodgers

5. The St. Louis Cardinals traded left-hand pitcher Steve Carlton to the Philadelphia Phillies on February 25, 1972.

a. True

b. False

6. What year did the Cardinals acquire Bruce Sutter from the Chicago Cubs?

a. 1978

b. 1979

c. 1980

d. 1981

7. At the trade deadline in 1997, the Cardinals traded right-hand pitcher Eric Ludwick, right-hand pitcher T.J. Mathews, and right-hand pitcher Blake Stein to the Oakland Athletics in exchange for _____.

   a. Mark McGwire
   b. Dennis Eckersley
   c. Rick Honeycutt
   d. Willie McGee

8. Which team traded outfielder Jim Edmonds to the Cardinals on March 23, 2000?

   a. Chicago Cubs
   b. San Diego Padres
   c. Anaheim Angels
   d. Milwaukee Brewers

9. On June 15, 1983, the Cardinals traded first baseman Keith Hernandez to the _____.

   a. Cleveland Indians
   b. New York Mets
   c. Detroit Tigers
   d. Houston Astros

10. The Cardinals acquired Scott Rolen from the Philadelphia Phillies on July 29, 2002.

    a. True
    b. False

11. On July 27, 2011, Cardinals center fielder Colby Lewis, left-hand pitcher Trever Miller, left-hand pitcher Brian

Tallet, and right-hand pitcher P.J. Walters were traded to the _____ in exchange for right-hand pitcher Octavio Dotel, right-hand pitcher Edwin Jackson, center fielder Corey Patterson, and left-hand pitcher Marc Rzepczynski.

a. Detroit Tigers
b. New York Yankees
c. Toronto Blue Jays
d. Tampa Bay Rays

12. The Cardinals have only made six trades each with the Arizona Diamondbacks and Colorado Rockies as of the end of the 2019 season.

a. True
b. False

13. How many trades have the Cardinals made with the Texas Rangers all time (as of the end of the 2019 season)?

a. 7
b. 10
c. 19
d. 25

14. The Cardinals have NEVER made a trade with the Chicago Cubs.

a. True
b. False

15. At the trade deadline in 2014, the St. Louis Cardinals traded Allen Craig and Joe Kelly to the _____

in exchange for John Lackey, Corey Littrell, and cash considerations.

a. Los Angeles Angels of Anaheim
b. Chicago Cubs
c. Miami Marlins
d. Boston Red Sox

16. On July 24, 2009, the Oakland Athletics traded _____ to the Cardinals in exchange for Clayton Mortensen, Shane Peterson, and Brett Wallace.

a. Colby Rasmus
b. David Freese
c. Matt Holliday
d. Kyle Lohse

17. How many trades have the St. Louis Cardinals made with the Toronto Blue Jays all time (as of the end of the 2019 season)?

a. 1
b. 5
c. 10
d. 15

18. On December 14, 2017, the St. Louis Cardinals traded _____ to the Oakland Athletics in exchange for Max Schrock and Yairo Munoz.

a. Stephen Piscotty
b. Jedd Gyorko
c. Tommy Pham
d. Matt Carpenter

19. The Cardinals have made ___ trades with the Colorado Rockies in franchise history (as of July 2020).

    a.  1

    b.  6

    c.  8

    d.  12

20. On May 8, 1966, the San Francisco Giants traded Orlando Cepeda to the St. Louis Cardinals in exchange for Ray Sadecki.

    a.  True

    b.  False

# QUIZ ANSWERS

1. C – Lou Brock

2. B – Ozzie Smith

3. B – False, Musial spent his entire career with the Cardinals.

4. C – Atlanta Braves

5. A – True

6. C – 1980

7. A – Mark McGwire

8. C – Anaheim Angels

9. B – New York Mets

10. A – True

11. C – Toronto Blue Jays

12. A – True

13. C – 19

14. B – False

15. D – Boston Red Sox

16. C – Matt Holliday

17. C – 10

18. A – Stephen Piscotty

19. B – 6

20. A – True

# DID YOU KNOW?

1. On October 13, 1974, the Cardinals traded 1971 National League MVP Joe Torre to the New York Mets. He managed the Mets only three years after the trade.

2. The St. Louis Cardinals have only made 19 trades with the Kansas City Royals all time (as of the end of the 2019 season).

3. On December 5, 2018, the Arizona Diamondbacks traded first baseman Paul Goldschmidt to the St. Louis Cardinals in exchange for Carson Kelly, Luke Weaver, Andy Young, and a 2019 Competitive Balance Round B Pick.

4. On April 11, 1954, the St. Louis Cardinals traded Enos Slaughter to the New York Yankees in exchange for Emil Tellinger, Bill Virdon, and Mel Wright.

5. On December 5, 1957, the St. Louis Cardinals acquired Curt Flood and Joe Taylor from the Cincinnati Redlegs in exchange for Marty Kutyna, Willard Schmidt, and Ted Wieand.

6. On December 8, 2015, the St. Louis Cardinals traded Jon Jay to the San Diego Padres in exchange for Jedd Gyorko and cash considerations.

7. On December 14, 2007, the St. Louis Cardinals traded Jim Edmonds to the San Diego Padres in exchange for David Freese. (He would come in handy during the 2011 World Series.)

8. The St. Louis Cardinals have only made three trades total with the Tampa Bay Rays (as of July 2020).

9. When the Cardinals traded Curt Flood to the Philadelphia Phillies in 1969, he refused to report to his new team.

10. On June 14, 1956, the St. Louis Cardinals traded Red Schoendienst, Jackie Brandt, Dick Littlefield, Bill Sarni, and players to be named later (PTBNL) to the New York Giants in exchange for Al Dark, Ray Katt, Don Liddle, Whitey Lockman, and cash considerations. The Cards sent Bob Stephenson and Gordon Jones to the Giants later in 1956 to complete the trade.

# CHAPTER 8:

# DRAFT DAY

## QUIZ TIME!

1. With the ___ overall pick in the 1st round of the 2008 MLB Draft, the St. Louis Cardinals selected right-hand pitcher Lance Lynn.

    a. 13th

    b. 20th

    c. 39th

    d. 8th

2. With the 5th overall pick in the 1st round of the 1998 MLB Draft, the St. Louis Cardinals selected _____.

    a. Ben Diggins

    b. J.D. Drew

    c. Adam Kennedy

    d. Nick Stocks

3. With the 22nd overall pick in 1st round of the 2011 MLB Draft, the St. Louis Cardinals selected second baseman Kolten Wong from _____.

a. Cal State, Fullerton

b. University of California - Los Angeles

c. Hawaii Pacific University

d. University of Hawaii

4. With the ___ overall pick in the 1st round of the 2012 MLB Draft, the St. Louis Cardinals selected right-hand pitcher Michael Wacha.

a. 19th

b. 3rd

c. 24th

d. 9th

5. With the 36th overall pick in the 1st round of the 2012 MLB Draft, the St. Louis Cardinals selected Stephen Piscotty from _____.

a. San Diego State University

b. Stanford University

c. Sacramento State University

d. University of California - Berkeley

6. Shortstop Ozzie Smith was drafted in the 7th round of the 1976 MLB Draft by the Detroit Tigers. He did not sign with the Tigers. He was then drafted again in the 4th round of the 1977 MLB Draft by the _____, whom he did sign with.

a. St. Louis Cardinals

b. Los Angeles Dodgers

c. New York Mets

d. San Diego Padres

7. Center fielder Jim Edmonds was drafted by the St. Louis Cardinals in the 7th round of the 1988 MLB Draft out of Diamond Bar High School.

    a. True

    b. False

8. Pitcher Adam Wainwright was drafted 29th overall in the 1st round of the 2000 MLB Draft by the _____.

    a. St. Louis Cardinals

    b. Texas Rangers

    c. Minnesota Twins

    d. Atlanta Braves

9. With the 15st overall pick in 1st round of the 1993 MLB Draft, the _____ selected right-hand pitcher Chris Carpenter.

    a. St. Louis Cardinals

    b. Tampa Bay Devil Rays

    c. Toronto Blue Jays

    d. Cincinnati Reds

10. David Freese was drafted by the St. Louis Cardinals in the 9th round of the 2006 MLB Draft.

    a. True

    b. False

11. In the 1st round of the 2009 MLB Draft, the St. Louis Cardinals selected right-hand pitcher _____ 19th overall.

a. Shelby Miller

b. Kyle Lohse

c. Joe Kelly

d. Jaime Garcia

12. Bryce Harper was drafted 1st overall in the 1st round of the 2010 MLB Draft by the St. Louis Cardinals.

a. True

b. False

13. Albert Pujols was drafted in the ____ round of the 1999 MLB Draft by the St. Louis Cardinals.

a. 1st

b. 3rd

c. 20th

d. 13th

14. The St. Louis Cardinals selected catcher Yadier Molina in the 4th round of the _____ MLB Draft.

a. 1999

b. 2000

c. 2001

d. 2002

15. Former Cardinals catcher/manager Mike Matheny was drafted by the Toronto Blue Jays in the 31st round of the 1988 MLB Draft but did not sign. He was drafted again in the 1991 MLB Draft in the 8th round by the _____.

a. St. Louis Cardinals

b. Kansas City Royals

c. Milwaukee Brewers

d. San Francisco Giants

16. Cardinals center fielder Dexter Fowler was drafted in the 14th round of the 2004 MLB Draft by the _____.

a. Chicago Cubs

b. Houston Astros

c. Minnesota Twins

d. Colorado Rockies

17. In the 21st round of the 2009 MLB Draft, the St. Louis Cardinals selected right-hand pitcher _____.

a. Trevor Rosenthal

b. Mike Leake

c. Tyson Ross

d. Carlos Martinez

18. The St. Louis Cardinals selected outfielder Jon Jay in the ____ round of the 2006 MLB Draft out of the University of Miami.

a. 1st

b. 2nd

c. 15th

d. 22nd

19. Former Cardinals left fielder Matt Holliday was drafted in the 7th round of the _____ MLB Draft by the Colorado Rockies.

a. 1995

b. 1996

c.  1998

d.  2000

20. Left-hand pitcher Mark Rzepczynski was drafted by the St. Louis Cardinals in the 5$^{th}$ round of the 2007 MLB Draft.

a.  True

b.  False

# QUIZ ANSWERS

1. C – 39th

2. B – J.D. Drew

3. D – University of Hawaii

4. A – 19th

5. B – Stanford University

6. D – San Diego Padres

7. B – False, The California Angels drafted Edmonds.

8. D – Atlanta Braves

9. C – Toronto Blue Jays

10. B – False, The San Diego Padres drafted Freese.

11. A – Shelby Miller

12. B – False, The Washington Nationals drafted Harper.

13. D – 13th

14. B – 2000

15. C – Milwaukee Brewers

16. D – Colorado Rockies

17. A – Trevor Rosenthal

18. B – 2nd

19. C – 1998

20. B – False, The Toronto Blue Jays drafted Rzepczynski.

# DID YOU KNOW?

1.  The St. Louis Cardinals selected outfielder Colby Rasmus 28th overall in the 1st round of the 2005 MLB Draft.

2.  The St. Louis Cardinals selected shortstop Pete Kozma 18th overall in the 1st round of the 2007 MLB Draft.

3.  The St. Louis Cardinals drafted Daniel Descalso in the 3rd round of the 2007 MLB Draft out of the University of California-Davis.

4.  The St. Louis Cardinals drafted Allen Craig in the 8th round of the 2006 MLB Draft out of the University of California-Berkeley.

5.  The St. Louis Cardinals drafted Skip Schumaker in the 5th round of the 2001 MLB Draft out of the University of California-Santa Barbara.

6.  The St. Louis Cardinals drafted right-hand pitcher Joe Kelly in the 3rd round of the 2009 MLB Draft out of the University of California-Riverside.

7.  Hall of Fame pitcher John Smoltz pitched in St. Louis for seven games in 2009. He was drafted by the Detroit Tigers in the 22nd round of the 1985 MLB Draft out of high school.

8.  The St. Louis Cardinals drafted Brendan Ryan in the 7th round of the 2003 MLB Draft out of Lewis-Clark State College.

9.  Former Cardinals outfielder Willie McGee was drafted by the Chicago White Sox in the 7th round of the 1976 MLB Draft but did not sign. He was drafted again in the 1st round, 15th overall by the New York Yankees in 1977.

10. Former Cardinals slugger Mark McGwire was drafted by the Montreal Expos in the 8th round of the 1981 MLB Draft out of high school, but he decided to attend college instead. He was then drafted by the Oakland Athletics in the 1st round, 10th overall in the 1984 MLB Draft out of USC.

# CHAPTER 9:

# ODDS & ENDS

## QUIZ TIME!

1. Bravo TV host Andy Cohen named his dog after which Cardinals pitcher?

    a. Bob Gibson

    b. Jason Isringhausen

    c. Adam Wainwright

    d. Michael Wacha

2. Former Cardinals manager Tony La Russa has a no-kill pet shelter in Walnut Creek, California, called Tony La Russa's Animal Rescue Foundation (ARF).

    a. True

    b. False

3. Which reality TV show did former Cardinal Jim Edmonds star on with his ex-wife Meghan?

    a. *90 Day Fiancé*

    b. *The Real Housewives of Orange County*

    c. *Survivor*

    d. *Vanderpump Rules*

4. Cardinal Ozzie Smith guest-starred in which of the following animated TV shows?

   a. *The Simpsons*
   b. *Bob's Burgers*
   c. *Family Guy*
   d. *American Dad*

5. When Mark McGwire played for the Oakland A's, he and his teammate _____ were considered the "Bash Brothers."

   a. Rickey Henderson
   b. Dave Henderson
   c. Jose Canseco
   d. Carney Lansford

6. Stan Musial made a guest appearance on a TV show called *Hee Haw*, where he played the _____.

   a. Piano
   b. Banjo
   c. Guitar
   d. Harmonica

7. Albert Pujols scored 100% on his U.S. citizenship test.

   a. True
   b. False

8. In retirement, former Cardinals pitcher Mark Mulder enjoys playing which of the following sports in his free time?

   a. Tennis
   b. Golf

c. Basketball

d. Hockey

9. Which sport does Jason Isringhausen's daughter Madolyn play currently at Tennessee Tech?

    a. Volleyball

    b. Softball

    c. Basketball

    d. Tennis

10. Former Cardinals slugger Mark McGwire began a coaching career after retirement from playing baseball. As of the end of the 2019 season, which team has he NOT coached for?

    a. San Diego Padres

    b. St. Louis Cardinals

    c. Oakland A's

    d. Los Angeles Dodgers

11. How many siblings did former Cardinals third baseman Ken Boyer have?

    a. 0

    b. 1

    c. 13

    d. 16

12. In his first college game, Albert Pujols hit a grand slam and turned an unassisted triple play.

    a. True

    b. False

13. What baseball-related item does Cardinals catcher Yadier Molina have tattooed on his right arm?

    a. A 2011 World Series trophy
    b. The MLB logo
    c. A catcher's mask
    d. A home plate

14. Which former Cardinal is now an analyst for MLB Network?

    a. Mark DeRosa
    b. Mark McGwire
    c. Ozzie Smith
    d. Lance Berkman

15. Where did Michael Wacha attend college?

    a. The University of Texas at Austin
    b. Texas A&M University
    c. Notre Dame University
    d. Vanderbilt University

16. Bengie Molina, Yadier's brother, is a color analyst for Cardinals Spanish radio broadcasts.

    a. True
    b. False

17. Which former Cardinals player is currently a game analyst for Cardinals TV broadcasts?

    a. Scott Rolen
    b. Mark McGwire
    c. Ozzie Smith
    d. Jim Edmonds

18. As of the end of the 2019 season, what is the only other MLB team Albert Pujols has played for besides the Cardinals?

    a. Los Angeles Angels of Anaheim
    b. Philadelphia Phillies
    c. Boston Red Sox
    d. Minnesota Twins

19. Who was the first Cardinal to throw a no-hitter?

    a. Bob Gibson
    b. Bob Forsch
    c. Ted Breitenstein
    d. Bud Smith

20. There has never been a perfect game thrown in Cardinals history.

    a. True
    b. False

# QUIZ ANSWERS

1. D – Michael Wacha

2. A – True

3. B – *The Real Housewives of Orange County*

4. A – *The Simpsons*, "Homer at the Bat" 1992 episode featuring multiple MLB players.

5. C – Jose Canseco

6. D – Harmonica

7. A – True

8. B – Golf

9. A – Volleyball

10. C – Oakland A's

11. C – 13

12. A – True

13. A – A 2011 World Series Trophy

14. A – Mark DeRosa

15. B – Texas A&M University

16. A – True

17. D – Jim Edmonds

18. A – Los Angeles Angels of Anaheim

19. C – Ted Breitenstein

20. A – True

# DID YOU KNOW?

1. Mark McGwire's brother Dan was a quarterback for the Seattle Seahawks and the Miami Dolphins in the 1990s. He was a 1$^{st}$ round draft choice out of San Diego State University. Mark's other brother is a bodybuilder, but they have supposedly not spoken to each other since around 2002.

2. Mark McGwire has appeared on a couple of TV shows in the past. He, like Ozzie Smith, made an appearance on *The Simpsons* in an episode called "Brother's Little Helper," and he was on an episode of *Mad About You* in which he played himself.

3. Some TV series that Stan Musial guest-starred on in the past were *What's My Line?*, *The Tonight Show Starring Johnny Carson*, *The Merv Griffin Show*, and *That Girl*.

4. Busch Stadium's groundbreaking took place on January 17, 2004. Its grass was installed on March 15, 2006. The first game played at Busch Stadium was on April 10, 2006, against the Milwaukee Brewers.

5. Adam Wainwright's twitter handle is @UncleCharlie50. His bio is where he claims his undying love for Chick-fil-A.

6. Busch Stadium has a section in the outfield seats called "Big Mac Land." It was once meant to honor Mark

McGwire, but due to his steroids scandal, it is now sponsored by McDonald's.

7. Cardinals catcher Yadier Molina owns a record label. It is called Molina Records.

8. A stretch of the Interstate 70 highway in St. Louis was once called the "Mark McGwire Highway." Now it is the "Mark Twain Expressway."

9. In over 30 years of managing, Tony La Russa was fired only once.

10. Tony La Russa is the third winningest baseball manager of all time in the MLB.

# CHAPTER 10:

# OUTFIELDERS

## QUIZ TIME!

1. Which team did former Cardinals outfielder Matt Holliday NOT play for during his MLB career?

    a. Colorado Rockies

    b. Oakland Athletics

    c. Atlanta Braves

    d. New York Yankees

2. Former Cardinals left fielder Lou Brock was never named to an MLB All-Star Game in his 19-year MLB career.

    a. True

    b. False

3. Which team did former Cardinals outfielder Willie McGee NOT play for during his 18-year MLB career?

    a. Boston Red Sox

    b. Oakland Athletics

    c. San Francisco Giants

    d. New York Mets

4. Former Cardinals outfielder Jon Jay did NOT hit a home run for the Cardinals during their 2011 World Series season.

   a. True
   b. False

5. How many Gold Glove Awards did former Cardinals outfielder Jim Edmonds receive during his 17-year MLB career?

   a. 8
   b. 4
   c. 9
   d. 10

6. How many games did former Cardinals outfielder Jason Heyward play in for the Cards during his lone season (2015) in St. Louis?

   a. 83
   b. 125
   c. 154
   d. 162

7. Joe Medwick played his entire 17-year MLB career with the Cardinals.

   a. True
   b. False

8. How many seasons did right fielder Enos Slaughter play for the Cardinals?

   a. 5
   b. 19

c. 6

d. 13

9. How many home runs did Dexter Fowler hit for the Cardinals during the 2019 season?

    a. 8

    b. 13

    c. 18

    d. 19

10. How many seasons did outfielder Jim Edmonds play for the St. Louis Cardinals?

    a. 8

    b. 7

    c. 6

    d. 11

11. Which team did former Cardinals right fielder J.D. Drew NOT play for during his 14-year MLB career?

    a. Oakland Athletics

    b. Los Angeles Dodgers

    c. Boston Red Sox

    d. Atlanta Braves

12. Carlos Beltran hit over 20 home runs in both of his seasons with the Cardinals (2012 and 2013).

    a. True

    b. False

13. How many hits did former Cardinals center fielder Curt Flood collect during the 1964 season?

a. 200

b. 211

c. 134

d. 99

14. What year did Stan Musial NOT play in the MLB due to military service?

    a. 1943

    b. 1944

    c. 1945

    d. 1946

15. How many stolen bases did former Cardinals left fielder Lou Brock collect during his 1974 season in St. Louis?

    a. 51

    b. 70

    c. 74

    d. 118

16. What year did former Cardinals outfielder Jim Edmonds win his sole Silver Slugger Award?

    a. 2000

    b. 2002

    c. 2004

    d. 2006

17. How many times was former Cardinals center fielder Curt Flood named to the MLB All-Star Game?

    a. 0 times

    b. 3 times

c. 6 times

d. 9 times

18. What was former Cardinals outfielder Willie McGee's batting average for the 1985 season?

a. .286

b. .291

c. .296

d. .353

19. How many years in a row did former Cardinals right fielder Enos Slaughter miss due to military service?

a. 1

b. 2

c. 3

d. 4

20. Stan Musial won the National League batting title seven times in his 22-year career with the Cardinals.

a. True

b. False

# QUIZ ANSWERS

1. C – Atlanta Braves

2. B – False, He was named All-Star six times.

3. D – New York Mets

4. B – False, Jay hit 10 home runs.

5. A – 8

6. C – 154

7. B – False, Medwick also played for the Brooklyn Dodgers, New York Giants, and Boston Braves.

8. D – 13

9. D – 19

10. A – 8

11. A – Oakland Athletics

12. A – True

13. B – 211

14. C – 1945

15. D – 118

16. C – 2004

17. B – 3 times

18. D – .353

19. C – 3

20. A – True

# DID YOU KNOW?

1. Stan Musial played all 22 seasons of his MLB career with the St. Louis Cardinals. By the end of his career, he had played 3,026 games for the Cards.

2. Lou Brock played 16 seasons of his 19-season MLB career with the St. Louis Cardinals. The only other MLB team he played for was the rival Chicago Cubs. He played a total of 2,289 games for the Cards.

3. Former Cardinals outfielder Willie McGee garnered many accolades during his 18-season MLB career, including MVP, named All-Star four times, three Gold Glove Awards, one Silver Slugger Award, named batting champion two times, and 1982 World Series champion.

4. Former Cardinals outfielder J.D. Drew has a brother, Stephen Drew, who also played in the MLB for the Arizona Diamondbacks, Oakland Athletics, Boston Red Sox, New York Yankees, and Washington Nationals.

5. Former Cardinals outfielder Enos Slaughter was named to the MLB All-Star Game 10 times during his 19-season MLB career. He was also a four-time World Series champion.

6. Former Cardinals center fielder Curt Flood was named All-Star three times, won seven Gold Glove Awards, and was a World Series champion twice. He played for the Cardinals for 12 seasons out of his 15-season MLB career.

7. Stan Musial's all-time stats include 475 home runs, 3,630 hits, and 1,951 RBI.

8. Lou Brock's all-time stats include 149 home runs, 3,023 hits, and 938 RBI.

9. Curt Flood's all-time stats include 85 home runs, 1,861 hits, and 636 RBI.

10. Jim Edmonds's all-time stats include 393 home runs, 1,949 hits, and 1,199 RBI.

# CHAPTER 11:

# INFIELDERS

## QUIZ TIME!

1. How many games did former Cardinals shortstop Ozzie Smith play in during his 15 seasons in St. Louis?

    a. 1,690

    b. 1,790

    c. 1,890

    d. 1,990

2. First baseman Albert Pujols played for the Cardinals for 11 seasons before he became an Angel.

    a. True

    b. False

3. How many home runs did former Cardinals first baseman Albert Pujols hit during his 11 seasons with the team?

    a. 212

    b. 445

    c. 333

    d. 429

4. Mark McGwire played for two teams during his 16-season MLB career, the Cardinals and the _____.

   a. Oakland Athletics
   b. San Diego Padres
   c. Baltimore Orioles
   d. Los Angeles Dodgers

5. Which MLB team did former Cardinals third baseman Ken Boyer NOT play for during his 15-season career?

   a. Chicago White Sox
   b. Los Angeles Dodgers
   c. Chicago Cubs
   d. New York Mets

6. How many seasons did Red Schoendienst play in the Major Leagues?

   a. 10
   b. 12
   c. 15
   d. 19

7. First baseman Keith Hernandez played his entire MLB career with the St. Louis Cardinals.

   a. True
   b. False

8. How many home runs did former Cardinal Lance Berkman hit during his two seasons with the team?

   a. 19
   b. 28

c. 33

d. 40

9. What was David Freese's batting average for his 2011 world championship season with the Cardinals?

a. .297

b. .323

c. .296

d. .260

10. During his 16-season career, former Cardinals first baseman Mark McGwire appeared in ___ MLB All-Star Games, won three Silver Slugger Awards and a Gold Glove Award, and was named the 1987 American League Rookie of the Year.

a. 3

b. 6

c. 12

d. 15

11. How many games did Cardinals first baseman Paul Goldschmidt play in for the Cards during the 2019 season?

a. 162

b. 105

c. 123

d. 161

12. Cardinals second baseman Kolten Wong stole 24 bases during the 2019 season.

a. True

b. False

13. As of the end of the 2019 season, how many times has Cardinals infielder Matt Carpenter been named an MLB All-Star?

    a. 0 times
    b. 1 time
    c. 3 times
    d. 5 times

14. Which team did former Cardinals infielder David Eckstein NOT play for during his 10-season MLB career?

    a. Los Angeles Angels of Anaheim
    b. Los Angeles Dodgers
    c. San Diego Padres
    d. Toronto Blue Jays

15. How many seasons did third baseman Scott Rolen play for the St. Louis Cardinals?

    a. 4
    b. 6
    c. 8
    d. 10

16. The most home runs that first baseman Albert Pujols hit in a single season during his time with the Cardinals was 49 in 2006.

    a. True
    b. False

17. How many home runs did first baseman Mark McGwire hit for the Cardinals during the 1998 season?

    a. 58
    b. 65
    c. 70
    d. 75

18. What year was Cardinals shortstop Ozzie Smith named the NLCS MVP?

    a. 1987
    b. 1985
    c. 1994
    d. 1996

19. Which team has former Cardinals infielder Jedd Gyorko NOT played for (as of the 2020 season) during his MLB career?

    a. Tampa Bay Rays
    b. San Diego Padres
    c. Los Angeles Dodgers
    d. Milwaukee Brewers

20. Former Cardinals infielder Adam Kennedy played for the Los Angeles Angels of Anaheim between his two stints with the St. Louis Cardinals.

    a. True
    b. False

# QUIZ ANSWERS

1. D – 1,990

2. A – True

3. B – 445

4. A – Oakland Athletics

5. C – Chicago Cubs

6. D – 19

7. B – False, Hernandez also played for the New York Mets and the Cleveland Indians.

8. C – 33

9. A – .297

10. C – 12

11. D – 161

12. A – True

13. C – 3 times

14. B – Los Angeles Dodgers

15. B – 6

16. A – True

17. C – 70

18. B – 1985

19. A – Tampa Bay Rays

20. A – True

# DID YOU KNOW?

1. Infielder Brendan Ryan played for the Cardinals for four seasons. He also played for the New York Yankees, Seattle Mariners, and Los Angeles Angels of Anaheim.

2. Second baseman Skip Schumaker played for the Cardinals for eight seasons and 810 games.

3. First baseman Albert Pujols played for the Cardinals for 11 seasons and is currently playing his ninth season with the Los Angeles Angels of Anaheim. As of the end of the 2019 season, he has 445 career home runs.

4. Former Cardinals first baseman Albert Pujols was named the 2001 National League Rookie of the Year.

5. Former Cardinals first baseman Will Clark also played for the San Francisco Giants, Baltimore Orioles, and Texas Rangers during his 15-season MLB career. He was known as "Will the Thrill."

6. During his 19-season MLB career, former Cardinals second baseman Red Schoendienst was named an MLB All-Star 10 times and was a World Series champion twice.

7. Cardinals first baseman Keith Hernandez was named an All-Star five times, won the World Series twice; won 11 Gold Glove Awards, two Silver Slugger Awards, and the 1979 NL batting title. He was also named National League MVP in 1979.

8. Cardinals second baseman Kolten Wong was named the 2014 National League Rookie of the Month in May of 2014. In his rookie season, he hit 12 home runs, had 42 RBI, and had a .249 batting average in 113 games.

9. Former Cardinals third baseman David Freese was named the 2011 World Series MVP. He played in all seven games, had eight hits and four runs, plus a home run and five walks in 23 at-bats.

10. Former Cardinals first baseman Mark McGwire was intentionally walked 150 times in his entire MLB career. Former Cardinals first baseman Albert Pujols has been intentionally walked 311 times in his career as of the end of the 2019 season.

# CHAPTER 12:

# PITCHERS & CATCHERS

## QUIZ TIME!

1. How many strikeouts did Bob Gibson record during his 1968 season with the Cardinals?

   a. 166

   b. 208

   c. 268

   d. 301

2. The most home runs that Yadier Molina has hit in a single season with the Cardinals is 22 (as of the end of the 2019 season).

   a. True

   b. False

3. Which pitcher has NOT pitched for BOTH the St. Louis Cardinals AND the Chicago Cubs in his MLB career?

   a. Dan Haren

   b. Rick Sutcliffe

   c. Mark Mulder

   d. John Lackey

4. Which former Cardinals manager was a catcher in their playing career?

   a. Tony La Russa
   b. Ken Boyer
   c. Charles Comiskey
   d. Mike Matheny

5. How many wins did pitcher Michael Wacha collect for the Cardinals in 2015?

   a. 17
   b. 12
   c. 7
   d. 6

6. How many saves did Jason Isringhausen record for the Cardinals during the 2004 season?

   a. 37
   b. 43
   c. 47
   d. 32

7. Cardinals catcher Mike Matheny was NEVER named to an MLB All-Star Game in his playing career.

   a. True
   b. False

8. Bob Gibson was awarded ___ Gold Gloves during his 17-season MLB career.

   a. 0
   b. 9

c. 5

d. 3

9. How many games did pitcher Shelby Miller start for the Cardinals during the 2015 season?

a. 31

b. 33

c. 20

d. 41

10. How many batters did Adam Wainwright face during his 2009 season with the Cardinals?

a. 898

b. 956

c. 970

d. 1,001

11. What one other MLB team did pitcher Mark Mulder play for during his playing career?

a. Atlanta Braves

b. Oakland A's

c. Los Angeles Dodgers

d. Texas Rangers

12. On September 17, 1968, the San Francisco Giants no-hit the Cardinals. The following day, Cardinals pitcher Ray Washburn no-hit the Giants.

a. True

b. False

13. How many games did pitcher Trevor Rosenthal appear in for the Cardinals in 2013?

    a. 68
    b. 72
    c. 74
    d. 76

14. How many Silver Slugger Awards did Cardinals pitcher Bob Forsch win during his 16-year MLB career?

    a. 0
    b. 1
    c. 2
    d. 3

15. How many MLB All-Star Games did former Cardinals catcher Ted Simmons appear in during his 21-year MLB career?

    a. 2
    b. 4
    c. 8
    d. 10

16. Cardinals pitcher Bruce Sutton never won a World Series during his 12-year career.

    a. True
    b. False

17. How many Gold Glove Awards did former Cardinals catcher Tony Peña win during his 18-year MLB career?

    a. 2
    b. 4

c. 5

d. 7

18. How many intentional walks did former Cardinals pitcher Omar Olivares issue during the 1993 season?

a. 0

b. 1

c. 5

d. 7

19. How many wild pitches did pitcher Matt Morris throw in his 1998 season with the Cardinals?

a. 0

b. 1

c. 3

d. 5

20. Cardinals pitcher Adam Wainwright has won one Silver Slugger Award in his career with the Cardinals (as of the end of the 2019 season).

a. True

b. False

# QUIZ ANSWERS

1. C – 268

2. A – True, Molina hit this milestone in 2012.

3. C – Mark Mulder

4. D – Mike Matheny

5. A – 17

6. C – 47

7. A – True

8. B – 9

9. B – 33

10. C – 970

11. B – Oakland A's

12. A – True

13. C – 74

14. D – 3

15. C – 8

16. B – False, Sutton played on the winning team in 1982.

17. B – 4

18. D – 7

19. C – 3

20. A – True

# DID YOU KNOW?

1. As of the 2020 season, catcher Yadier Molina has been playing for the St. Louis Cardinals for 17 seasons.

2. Just a few of the many accolades Cardinals pitcher Bob Gibson won during his 17-year MLB career include MVP, two Cy Young Awards, named an All-Star nine times, named World Series MVP twice, two World Series championships, nine Gold Glove Awards, and an ERA title. He spent all of his 17 years in the MLB with the Cardinals.

3. Cardinals pitcher Bruce Sutter also won many accolades during his 12-year MLB career, including a Cy Young Award, named an All-Star six times, a World Series championship, and four Rolaids Relief Pitcher of the Year Awards.

4. Cardinals pitcher Bob Gibson won a whopping 23 games for St. Louis in 1970. He only lost seven games that year and threw 23 complete games. His ERA was not as good as it was in 1968, though, when it was only 1.12!

5. As of the end of the 2019 season, the most recent no-hitter in Cardinals history was on September 3, 2001, when Cards pitcher Bud Smith no-hit the Padres in San Diego.

6. No pitcher has ever thrown a perfect game for the Cardinals in franchise history (as of the end of the 2019 season).

7. Bob Forsch is the only pitcher in franchise history to throw multiple no-hitters for the team. He no-hit the Philadelphia Phillies on April 16, 1978, and the Montreal Expos on September 26, 1983.

8. Jamie Moyer pitched only one season for the St. Louis Cardinals. During his 25-season MLB career, he also played for the Texas Rangers, Colorado Rockies, Seattle Mariners, Chicago Cubs, Philadelphia Phillies, Baltimore Orioles, and Boston Red Sox. In those 25 years, he made the MLB All-Star Game only once, in 2003 with the Mariners.

9. On August 14, 1971, Cardinals pitcher Bob Gibson threw a no-hitter against the Pittsburgh Pirates. It was the first no-hitter thrown in Pittsburgh in 64 years. It was also the no-hitter with the largest margin of victory in franchise history. The Cardinals won the game 11-0.

10. The Cardinals have had 10 no-hitters in franchise history (as of the end of the 2019 season). Each of the 10 was against a different MLB team. So far, they have no-hit the Louisville Colonels, Boston Braves, Brooklyn Dodgers, Cincinnati Reds, San Francisco Giants, Pittsburgh Pirates, Philadelphia Phillies, Montreal Expos, Arizona Diamondbacks, and the San Diego Padres.

# CHAPTER 13:

# WORLD SERIES

## QUIZ TIME!

1. How many World Series have the St. Louis Cardinals won in franchise history (as of 2019)?

    a. 10
    b. 11
    c. 12
    d. 14

2. How many NL pennants have the St. Louis Cardinals won (as of 2019)?

    a. 19
    b. 18
    c. 15
    d. 12

3. Which team did the St. Louis Cardinals face in the 2011 World Series?

    a. Houston Astros
    b. New York Yankees

c. Oakland Athletics

d. Texas Rangers

4. Which team did the St. Louis Cardinals face in the 2006 World Series?

   a. Tampa Bay Devil Rays

   b. Los Angeles Angels of Anaheim

   c. Detroit Tigers

   d. Minnesota Twins

5. As of the end of the 2019 season, the St. Louis Cardinals have had three wild card berths in franchise history. In which season did the Cardinals NOT win a wild card berth?

   a. 2001

   b. 2011

   c. 2012

   d. 2013

6. How many games did the 2011 World Series go?

   a. 4

   b. 5

   c. 6

   d. 7

7. Darrell Porter was named the 1982 World Series MVP.

   a. True

   b. False

8. Who was the manager when the Cardinals won the World Series in 1964?

a. Tony La Russa

b. Red Schoendienst

c. Johnny Keane

d. Whitey Herzog

9. How many games did the 2006 World Series go?

a. 4

b. 5

c. 6

d. 7

10. Which pitcher started Game 1 of the 2006 World Series for the Cardinals?

a. Anthony Reyes

b. Mark Mulder

c. Chris Carpenter

d. Jason Marquis

11. Which pitcher started Game 1 of the 2011 World Series for the Cardinals?

a. Kyle Lohse

b. Chris Carpenter

c. Edwin Jackson

d. Jaime Garcia

12. The Cardinals beat the New York Yankees in the 1926 World Series.

a. True

b. False

13. What team did the St. Louis Cardinals beat in the 1944 World Series?

    a. Boston Red Sox
    b. Chicago White Sox
    c. St. Louis Browns
    d. Philadelphia Athletics

14. Who was the only Cardinals pitcher to record a save in the 2006 World Series?

    a. Adam Wainwright
    b. Chris Carpenter
    c. Tyler Johnson
    d. Jeff Weaver

15. Which Cardinal did NOT hit a home run in the 2011 World Series?

    a. Albert Pujols
    b. Yadier Molina
    c. Lance Berkman
    d. Allen Craig

16. The St. Louis Cardinals won their first National League Central Division championship title in 1996.

    a. True
    b. False

17. Which team did the St. Louis Cardinals play and beat in the 2012 National League wild card game?

    a. San Diego Padres
    b. Colorado Rockies

c. Washington Nationals

d. Atlanta Braves

18. Which team did the St. Louis Cardinals play in the 1982 World Series?

a. New York Yankees

b. Milwaukee Brewers

c. Oakland A's

d. Boston Red Sox

19. What was the final score of Game 7 of the 2011 World Series?

a. Rangers 2, Cardinals 3

b. Rangers 3, Cardinals 2

c. Rangers 2, Cardinals 6

d. Rangers 6, Cardinals 2

20. Which Cardinal was named the 1967 World Series MVP?

a. Bob Gibson

b. Orlando Cepeda

c. Lou Brock

d. Roger Maris

# QUIZ ANSWERS

1. B – 11

2. A – 19

3. D – Texas Rangers

4. C – Detroit Tigers

5. D – 2013

6. D – 7

7. A – True

8. C – Johnny Keane

9. B – 5

10. A – Anthony Reyes

11. B – Chris Carpenter

12. A – True

13. C – St. Louis Browns

14. A – Adam Wainwright

15. B – Yadier Molina

16. A – True

17. D – Atlanta Braves

18. B – Milwaukee Brewers

19. C – Rangers 2, Cardinals 6

20. A – Bob Gibson

# DID YOU KNOW?

1. The Cardinals beat the New York Yankees in the 1926 World Series. They beat the Philadelphia Athletics in the 1931 World Series, the Detroit Tigers in the 1934 World Series, the Yankees again in 1942, the St. Louis Browns in 1944, the Boston Red Sox in 1946, the Yankees for a third time in 1964, the Red Sox for a second time in 1967, the Milwaukee Brewers (who were in the American League at the time) in 1982, the Detroit Tigers in 2006, and finally the Texas Rangers in the 2011 World Series.

2. The 1926, 1931, 1934, 1946, 1964, 1967, 1982, and the 2011 World Series all went seven games.

3. David Eckstein and Scott Rolen tied for the most hits for the Cardinals in the 2006 World Series, with 8 each. Yadier Molina had 7 hits in the 2006 World Series.

4. Lance Berkman had the most hits for the Cardinals in the 2011 World Series, with 11. David Freese and Yadier Molina tied for the second most hits with 8 each.

5. George Hendrick, Dane Iorg, and Lonnie Smith all tied for the most hits for the Cardinals in the 1982 World Series, with 9 each.

6. Bruce Sutter recorded the most strikeouts for the Cardinals in the 1982 World Series, with 6.

7. Chris Carpenter recorded the most strikeouts for the Cardinals in the 2006 World Series, with 6. He also

recorded the most strikeouts for the Cardinals in the 2011 World Series, with 13.

8. The 2011 World Series began on October 19 at Busch Stadium and ended on October 28, also at Busch Stadium.

9. The 2006 World Series began on October 21 at Comerica Park in Detroit and ended on October 27 at Busch Stadium.

10. The 1982 World Series began on October 12 at Busch Stadium and ended on October 20, also at Busch Stadium.

# CHAPTER 14:

# HEATED RIVALRIES

## QUIZ TIME!

1. Which team does NOT play in the National League Central with the Cardinals?

   a. Pittsburgh Pirates
   b. Chicago Cubs
   c. Philadelphia Phillies
   d. Milwaukee Brewers

2. The Cardinals-Cubs rivalry is often referred to as the Route 66 Rivalry and the I-55 Rivalry.

   a. True
   b. False

3. The Cardinals and Chicago Cubs have met once in the MLB playoffs. The Cubs won three games to one. What year did this NLDS matchup occur?

   a. 1995
   b. 2004
   c. 2012
   d. 2015

4. In June 2020, the Cardinals and Cubs were supposed to play a series internationally in _____, but the series was canceled due to the COVID-19 Pandemic.

   a. Paris, France
   b. Barcelona, Spain
   c. London, England
   d. Dublin, Ireland

5. Which Cardinal and Cub had a 1998 rivalry to chase the MLB home run record?

   a. J.D. Drew and Sammy Sosa
   b. Mark McGwire and Sammy Sosa
   c. Mark McGwire and Mark Grace
   d. Delino DeShields and Mark Grace

6. The Cardinals have 11 World Series championships as of the end of the 2019 season. How many do the Cubs have?

   a. 1
   b. 2
   c. 3
   d. 6

7. The Cubs and Cardinals shared Wrigley Field for a short period, which was a big part of their rivalry.

   a. True
   b. False

8. On May 15, 1960, which pitcher threw a no-hitter against the Cardinals in his debut with the Cubs?

a. Bob Anderson

b. Moe Drabowsky

c. John Goetz

d. Don Cardwell

9. Which player has NOT played for BOTH the Cubs AND the Cardinals?

a. Ryan Theriot

b. Ted Simmons

c. Lee Smith

d. Lou Brock

10. Before the 2019 season, which Cub is quoted as saying, "Who would want to play in St. Louis? So boring."

a. Kris Bryant

b. Anthony Rizzo

c. Javier Báez

d. Kyle Schwarber

11. In 2005, the Cubs' Derrek Lee and Cardinals' Albert Pujols were locked in a tight NL MVP race. Who ended up winning the honor that year?

a. Pujols

b. Lee

c. It was a tie.

d. Neither of them

12. Ryan Theriot was acquired by the Cardinals in 2010 and was quoted as saying he was "finally on the right side of the Cardinals-Cubs rivalry."

a. True

b. False

13. The Cardinals have won 19 National League pennants. How many have the Chicago Cubs won (as of the end of the 2019 season)?

    a. 5
    b. 11
    c. 13
    d. 17

14. Which of the players below did NOT play for BOTH the St. Louis Cardinals AND the Chicago Cubs?

    a. Mordecai Brown
    b. Bobby Bonds
    c. Orlando Cepeda
    d. Dizzy Dean

15. Which of the players below did NOT play for BOTH the St. Louis Cardinals AND the Chicago Cubs?

    a. Mike Matheny
    b. Jim Edmonds
    c. Dennis Eckersley
    d. Joe Girardi

16. The Cardinals and Cubs met in the World Series when the Cardinals were the "Browns" and a member of the American Association. They tied in 1885, and St. Louis won in 1886.

    a. True
    b. False

17. Which of the players below did NOT play for BOTH the St. Louis Cardinals AND the Texas Rangers?

    a. Lance Berkman
    b. Brendan Ryan
    c. Bobby Bonds
    d. Will Clark

18. The St. Louis Cardinals defeated the Texas Rangers in the 2011 World Series. How many World Series championships do the Rangers have?

    a. 3
    b. 2
    c. 1
    d. 0

19. The St. Louis Cardinals drafted pitcher Derek Holland, who was a member of the Texas Rangers during the 2011 World Series.

    a. True
    b. False

20. Ben Zobrist, who grew up as a Cardinals fan, won World Series MVP for the Cubs in 2016.

    a. True
    b. False

# QUIZ ANSWERS

1.  C – Philadelphia Phillies

2.  A – True

3.  D – 2015

4.  C – London, England

5.  B – Mark McGwire and Sammy Sosa

6.  C – 3

7.  B – False

8.  D – Don Cardwell

9.  B – Ted Simmons

10. A – Kris Bryant

11. A – Pujols

12. A – True

13. D – 17

14. C – Orlando Cepeda

15. A – Mike Matheny

16. A – True

17. B – Brendan Ryan

18. D – 0

19. B – False, Holland was drafted by the Rangers.

20. A – True

# DID YOU KNOW?

1. The first meeting between the Cardinals and Cubs took place on April 12, 1892, at Sportsman's Park in St. Louis.

2. The Cubs' Hack Wilson jumped into the stands to attack a heckling Cardinals fan in 1928. Five thousand fans swarmed the field in a riot, and the fan sued Wilson for $20,000.

3. The Cardinals/Cubs rivalry was heightened even more when Dexter Fowler decided to sign with the Cardinals the year after the Cubs won the 2016 World Series Championship.

4. The Cubs/Cardinals rivalry is an important geographical stamp in the Netflix show *Ozark*. A couple of direct quotes from the show are: "I was raised to hate the Cubs" and "I was raised to hate the Cardinals."

5. Hall-of-Famer Rogers Hornsby holds several single-season hitting records for both the Cardinals and the Cubs.

6. The current regular-season record of the Cardinals-Cubs rivalry is Cubs 1,239-Cardinals 1,181.

7. The largest victory in Cardinals-Cubs series history was on April 16, 1912, when the Cardinals beat Chicago 20-5.

8. The longest win streak in Cardinals-Cubs series history is when the Cardinals won 14 in a row from April 21, 1944, to September 7, 1944.

9. In his book, *Before They Were Cardinals*, Jon David Cash speculates that the economic trade rivalry between the cities of Chicago and St. Louis led to the formation of the St. Louis Brown Stockings (Cardinals) in 1875 to compete with the Chicago White Stockings (Cubs).

10. In his book, *Ten Nights in August*, Buzz Bissinger compared the Cardinals-Cubs rivalry to the Red Sox-Yankees rivalry. "The Red Sox and Yankees is a tabloid-filled soap opera about money and ego and sound bites. But the Cubs and Cardinals are about...geography and territorial rights."

# CHAPTER 15:

# THE AWARDS SECTION

## QUIZ TIME!

1. Who is the only other Cardinals pitcher besides Bob Gibson to win a Cy Young Award?

   a. Mark Mulder

   b. Adam Wainwright

   c. Chris Carpenter

   d. Jason Isringhausen

2. No Cardinals manager has ever won the National League Manager of the Year Award.

   a. True

   b. False

3. Who is the only Cardinals player to win a Platinum Glove Award? (He has won four.)

   a. Yadier Molina

   b. Jim Edmonds

   c. Ozzie Smith

   d. Albert Pujols

4.  Which Cardinal most recently won the NL Rookie of the Year Award (as of the end of the 2019 season)?

    a.  Wally Moon
    b.  Bake McBride
    c.  Todd Worrell
    d.  Albert Pujols

5.  How many Gold Glove Awards did Ozzie Smith win during his career?

    a.  11
    b.  2
    c.  6
    d.  12

6.  Which Cardinal won the World Series MVP Award in 2011?

    a.  Yadier Molina
    b.  David Freese
    c.  Albert Pujols
    d.  Matt Holliday

7.  No Cardinals player has ever won a Hank Aaron Award.

    a.  True
    b.  False

8.  Which Cardinals player was named the DHL Hometown Hero (voted by MLB fans as the most outstanding player in franchise history)?

    a.  Yadier Molina
    b.  Ozzie Smith

c. Stan Musial

d. Bob Gibson

9. How many NL Triple Crowns did Rogers Hornsby win?

   a. 0

   b. 1

   c. 2

   d. 3

10. Which Cardinal was named NLCS MVP in 2013?

    a. Jon Jay

    b. Adam Wainwright

    c. Carlos Beltran

    d. Michael Wacha

11. Which Cardinal won the 1967 NL MVP Award?

    a. Ken Boyer

    b. Orlando Cepeda

    c. Joe Torre

    d. Bob Gibson

12. Mark McGwire NEVER won a Silver Slugger Award during his career with the Cardinals.

    a. True

    b. False

13. Which Cardinal was named World Series MVP in 2006?

    a. David Eckstein

    b. Albert Pujols

    c. Scott Rolen

    d. Mark Mulder

14. Which Cardinals player has NEVER won an MLB Heart & Hustle Award?

    a. David Eckstein
    b. Harrison Bader
    c. Albert Pujols
    d. Yadier Molina

15. How many Gold Glove Awards did Jim Edmonds win as a member of the St. Louis Cardinals?

    a. 2
    b. 4
    c. 6
    d. 9

16. No Cardinals player has ever won the Home Run Derby.

    a. True
    b. False

17. Which Cardinals pitcher won a Silver Slugger Award in 2017?

    a. Adam Wainwright
    b. Lance Lynn
    c. Michael Wacha
    d. Trevor Rosenthal

18. Which Cardinal was named World Series MVP more than once?

    a. David Eckstein
    b. Bob Gibson
    c. David Freese
    d. Darrell Porter

19. How many Gold Glove Awards has Yadier Molina won so far in his career (as of the end of the 2019 season)?

    a. 3
    b. 6
    c. 9
    d. 11

20. Mark McGwire won the National League MVP Award in 1998.

    a. True
    b. False

# QUIZ ANSWERS

1. C – Chris Carpenter

2. B – False, Whitey Herzog, Tony La Russa, and Mike Schildt have received it.

3. A – Yadier Molina

4. D – Albert Pujols (2001)

5. A – 11

6. B – David Freese

7. B – False, Albert Pujols (2003, 2009)

8. C – Stan Musial

9. C – 2

10. D – Michael Wacha

11. B – Orlando Cepeda

12. B – False, McGwire won a Silver Slugger in 1998.

13. A – David Eckstein

14. D – Yadier Molina

15. C – 6 (consecutively from 2000 to 2005)

16. A – True

17. A – Adam Wainwright

18. B – Bob Gibson (1964, 1967)

19. C – 9

20. B – False, Sammy Sosa received this award.

# DID YOU KNOW?

1. Both Stan Musial and Albert Pujols won the National League MVP Award with the Cardinals three times each: Musial in 1943, 1946, and 1948; Pujols in 2005, 2008, and 2009.

2. Bob Gibson won two Cy Young Awards with the Cardinals, in 1968 and 1970.

3. Mark McGwire only won one Silver Slugger Award during his time with the Cardinals in 1998. He never won a Gold Glove with the Cards.

4. Four Cardinals have won a Roberto Clemente Award: Ozzie Smith in 1995, Albert Pujols in 2008, Carlos Beltran in 2013, and Yadier Molina in 2018.

5. Two Cardinals have won ESPN ESPY Awards for Best Major League Baseball Player. Mark McGwire won in 1999 and Albert Pujols in 2005, 2006, 2009, and 2010.

6. Six Cardinals have won the Lou Gehrig Memorial Award: Stan Musial in 1957, Ken Boyer in 1964, Lou Brock in 1977, Ozzie Smith in 1989, Mark McGwire in 1999, and Albert Pujols in 2009.

7. Four Cardinals broadcasters are Ford C. Frick Award recipients: Jack Buck, Harry Caray, Joe Garagiola, and Milo Hamilton.

8. Three Cardinals players have won NL Triple Crowns: Tip

O'Neill in 1887, Rogers Hornsby in 1922 and 1925, and Joe Medwick in 1937.

9. Although Tony La Russa is the Cardinals' winningest manager, he only won one NL Manager of the Year Award with the team, in 2002.

10. The first Cardinals player to win a Gold Glove was Ken Boyer in 1958.

# CHAPTER 16:

# THE GATEWAY TO THE WEST

## QUIZ TIME!

1. Which popular soda was created in St. Louis?

    a. Root beer

    b. 7UP

    c. Coca-Cola

    d. Mountain Dew

2. St. Louis was the first American city to host the Olympics.

    a. True

    b. False

3. What sauce does St. Louis consume the most per capita compared to every other U.S. city?

    a. Honey mustard

    b. Ketchup

    c. Ranch

    d. BBQ sauce

4. Who is St. Louis named after?

a. Louis Tomlinson

b. Louis Armstrong

c. King Louis IX

d. King Louis XVI

5. The founder of which social media platform was born in St. Louis?

a. Twitter

b. Facebook

c. Instagram

d. Snapchat

6. What is the name of the 630-foot monument in St Louis?

a. Golden Gate Bridge

b. Liberty Bell

c. The Bean

d. The Gateway Arch

7. Peanut butter was invented in St. Louis.

a. True

b. False

8. Which beer brewing company has called St. Louis home since 1852?

a. Coors

b. Budweiser

c. Anheuser-Busch

d. Corona

9. What is the name of the St. Louis NHL team?

a. St. Louis Cowboys

b. St. Louis Blues

c. St. Louis Sharks

d. St. Louis Bucks

10. What year was the City of St. Louis founded?

    a. 1874

    b. 1774

    c. 1764

    d. 1864

11. Which horror movie is based on true events that happened in St. Louis?

    a. *The Exorcist*

    b. *Child's Play*

    c. *Nightmare on Elm Street*

    d. *Psycho*

12. Iced tea was invented in St. Louis at the World's Fair in 1904.

    a. True

    b. False

13. Missouri is known as the _____.

    a. Golden State

    b. Bluegrass State

    c. Show-Me State

    d. Treasure State

14. Which popular medicine was created in St. Louis?

a. Tylenol

b. Delsym

c. Pepto-Bismol

d. Tums

15. What is the name of the arena that the St. Louis Blues of the NHL call home?

a. SAP Center

b. Nationwide Arena

c. Enterprise Center

d. Little Caesars Arena

16. Kindergarten began in St. Louis.

a. True

b. False

17. What county is St. Louis located in?

a. St. Louis County

b. Audrain County

c. Pemiscot County

d. Dunklin County

18. Busch Stadium is located 17.5 miles from St. Louis Lambert International Airport. What is St. Louis Lambert International Airport's code?

a. SLL

b. SLA

c. SLI

d. STL

19. St. Louis was formerly known as the largest _____ manufacturing center in the world.

   a. Coffee
   b. Shoe
   c. Paper
   d. Soap

20. St. Louis is known for gooey butter cake, toasted ravioli, and Provel cheese.

   a. True
   b. False

# QUIZ ANSWERS

1. B – 7UP

2. A – True

3. D – BBQ sauce

4. C – King Louis IX

5. A – Twitter

6. D – The Gateway Arch

7. A – True

8. C – Anheuser-Busch

9. B – St. Louis Blues

10. C – 1764

11. A – *The Exorcist*

12. A – True

13. C – Show-Me State

14. D – Tums

15. C – Enterprise Center

16. A – True

17. A – St. Louis County

18. D – STL

19. B – Shoe

20. A – True

# DID YOU KNOW?

1. The ice cream cone was invented in St. Louis.

2. The 1904 World's Fair was hosted in St. Louis.

3. The first interstate highway was built in St. Louis.

4. The Panera Bread chain began in St. Louis in 1993 under the name St. Louis Bread Company. It still goes by this name in the St. Louis area.

5. The Secret Service has forbidden all U.S. presidents from ascending the Gateway Arch for security reasons.

6. St. Louis has the most free tourist attractions in the U.S. other than Washington, D.C. The St. Louis Zoo, Art Museum, History Museum, Museum of Westward Expansion, Busch Brewery, Sculpture Park, and Citygarden are all free of charge.

7. St. Louis has the second biggest and best zoo in America behind the San Diego Zoo.

8. St. Louis University is the oldest university west of the Mississippi River.

9. The Anheuser-Busch brewery in St. Louis is the largest beer-producing plant in the United States.

10. Some of the most famous people from St. Louis include John Goodman, Jon Hamm, Andy Cohen, Nelly, Cedric the Entertainer, Ellie Kemper, Doris Roberts, Maya

Angelou, Chuck Berry, Yogi Berra, Kevin Nealon, Sterling K. Brown, Harry Caray, T.S. Eliot, Vincent Price, Miles Davis, Jenna Fischer, Joe Buck, Sheryl Crowe, and Ozzie Smith.

# CHAPTER 17:

# THE WIZARD OF OZ

## QUIZ TIME!

1. Where was Ozzie Smith born?

    a. St. Louis, Missouri

    b. Mobile, Alabama

    c. Oakland, California

    d. New Orleans, Louisiana

2. Ozzie Smith's first name is Osborne.

    a. True

    b. False

3. Ozzie Smith played for the Cardinals and one other team during his 19-year MLB career. What other MLB team did he play for?

    a. New York Mets

    b. Oakland A's

    c. Los Angeles Dodgers

    d. San Diego Padres

4. What year was Ozzie Smith born?

    a. 1949

    b. 1958

    c. 1954

    d. 1951

5. What uniform number did Ozzie Smith wear as a member of the Cardinals?

    a. 1

    b. 2

    c. 11

    d. 12

6. Ozzie Smith's son, Nikko, competed on which reality television show in 2005?

    a. *Survivor*

    b. *The Bachelorette*

    c. *American Idol*

    d. *Big Brother*

7. In 2012, Ozzie Smith sold all of his Gold Gloves at an auction for over $500,000.

    a. True

    b. False

8. Before the start of games, Ozzie Smith would do a _____ on his way out to the shortstop position.

    a. Push-up

    b. Backflip

    c. Bridge

    d. Jumping jack

9. Where did Ozzie Smith attend high school?

    a. Locke High School
    b. Bell High School
    c. Benjamin Franklin High School
    d. Los Angeles High School

10. How many All-Star Games was Ozzie Smith named to in his 19-year MLB career?

    a. 12
    b. 13
    c. 15
    d. 18

11. How many Gold Glove Awards did Ozzie Smith win during his 19-year MLB career?

    a. 9
    b. 11
    c. 13
    d. 14

12. Ozzie Smith hosted *This Week in Baseball* from 1997 to 1998.

    a. True
    b. False

13. What year was Ozzie Smith inducted into the National Baseball Hall of Fame?

    a. 1999
    b. 2000
    c. 2001
    d. 2002

14. How many World Series did Ozzie Smith win during his 19-year career?

    a. 0
    b. 1
    c. 2
    d. 3

15. What year did Ozzie Smith's playing career end?

    a. 2012
    b. 1996
    c. 2014
    d. 2005

16. At the end of Smith's career, he had tension with his manager Tony La Russa.

    a. True
    b. False

17. What year did Ozzie Smith make his MLB debut?

    a. 1980
    b. 1988
    c. 1970
    d. 1978

18. What year was Ozzie Smith named NLCS MVP?

    a. 1982
    b. 1987
    c. 1985
    d. 1996

19. Where did Ozzie Smith attend college?

    a. Cal State, Fullerton

    b. San Diego State University

    c. UCLA

    d. Cal Poly-San Louis Obispo

20. Ozzie Smith won more than one Silver Slugger Award.

    a. True

    b. False

# QUIZ ANSWERS

1. B – Mobile, Alabama

2. A – True

3. D – San Diego Padres

4. C – 1954

5. A – 1

6. C – *American Idol*

7. A – True

8. B – Backflip

9. A – Locke High School

10. C – 15

11. C – 13

12. A – True

13. D – 2002

14. B – 1

15. B – 1996

16. A – True

17. D – 1978

18. C – 1985

19. D – Cal Poly-San Louis Obispo

20. B – False, He won just one in 1987.

# DID YOU KNOW?

1. Ozzie Smith was drafted by the Detroit Tigers in the 7th round of the 1976 MLB Draft but did not sign with the team. He was drafted again in the 4th round the following year by the San Diego Padres, whom he ultimately signed with out of college.

2. Ozzie Smith learned to switch-hit from his coach at Cal Poly, Berdy Harr. At Cal Poly, he established school career records in both at-bats and stolen bases.

3. Ozzie Smith did not work for the Cardinals until after Tony La Russa retired from managing the team. Once he retired in 2011, Smith began a stint as a special instructor at spring training.

4. Ozzie Smith was named to the National Baseball Hall of Fame with 91.7% of the vote in his first year of eligibility.

5. Ozzie Smith wrote a children's book called Hello Freebird that was released in 2006.

6. In 2008, Ozzie Smith launched his own brand of salad dressing.

7. Ozzie Smith was named to the St. Louis Cardinals Hall of Fame Museum in 2014, its inaugural year.

8. Ozzie Smith played The Wizard in the St. Louis Municipal Opera's 2001 production of The Wizard of Oz.

9. Ozzie Smith only hit 28 home runs in his entire 19-year MLB career.

10. Back in 1998, Ozzie Smith opened a sports bar called Ozzie's.

# CHAPTER 18:

# YADI

## QUIZ TIME!

1. Where was Yadier Molina born?

    a. Bayamon, Puerto Rico

    b. San Juan, Puerto Rico

    c. Santo Domingo, Dominican Republic

    d. Havana, Cuba

2. Yadier Molina's brothers, Bengie and José, also played catcher in the MLB.

    a. True

    b. False

3. What other MLB team has Yadier Molina played for in his career (as of the end of the 2019 season)?

    a. Tampa Bay Rays

    b. Seattle Mariners

    c. Arizona Diamondbacks

    d. He has only ever played for the Cardinals.

4. When was Yadier Molina born?

    a. July 31, 1983
    b. July 13, 1982
    c. July 13, 1983
    d. July 31, 1982

5. As of the end of the 2019 season, how many Gold Glove Awards has Yadier Molina won?

    a. 3
    b. 6
    c. 9
    d. 10

6. As of the end of the 2019 season, how many World Series championships has Yadier Molina won with the Cardinals?

    a. 0
    b. 1
    c. 2
    d. 4

7. As of the end of the 2019 season, Yadier Molina has won four Platinum Glove Awards, which is an MLB record.

    a. True
    b. False

8. As of the end of the 2019 season, how many MLB All-Star Games has Yadier Molina been named to?

    a. 14
    b. 6
    c. 12
    d. 9

9. What year did Yadier Molina make his MLB debut with the Cardinals?

   a. 2002

   b. 2004

   c. 2006

   d. 2008

10. What year did Yadier Molina win a Silver Slugger Award?

   a. 2011

   b. 2012

   c. 2013

   d. 2014

11. How many National League titles has Yadier Molina won with the Cardinals (as of the end of the 2019 season)?

   a. 4

   b. 5

   c. 6

   d. 7

12. Yadier Molina played on the Cardinals with both of his brothers as his backups in 2009.

   a. True

   b. False

13. Yadier Molina is a huge fan of which NHL team?

   a. San Jose Sharks

   b. Los Angeles Kings

   c. Detroit Red Wings

   d. St. Louis Blues

14. What is the name of Yadier Molina's charity foundation?

    a. Fundación 4 (Foundation 4)
    b. Yadier Molina Familia Foundation (Yadier Molina Family Foundation)
    c. The Yadi Foundation
    d. The Molina Brothers Foundation

15. What uniform number did Yadier Molina wear during his first two seasons with the Cardinals?

    a. 4
    b. 41
    c. 14
    d. 44

16. Yadier Molina was drafted by the Anaheim Angels in the 4th round of the 2000 MLB Draft.

    a. True
    b. False

17. How many silver medals has Yadier Molina won as a member of Team Puerto Rico?

    a. 0
    b. 1
    c. 2
    d. 3

18. Where did Yadier Molina attend high school?

    a. Escuela Superior Lino Padron Rivera
    b. Emilio R. Delgado High School
    c. Carlos Gonzalez High School
    d. Ladislao Martinez High School

19. As of the end of the 2019 season, Yadier Molina has appeared on five National League MVP Ballots. How many times has he been named NL MVP?

    a.  5
    b.  3
    c.  1
    d.  0

20. All three of the Molina brothers, Yadier, Bengie, and José, have won at least one World Series championship, making them the only trio of brothers to accomplish this in MLB history.

    a.  True
    b.  False

# QUIZ ANSWERS

1. A – Bayamon, Puerto Rico

2. A – True

3. D – He has only ever played for the Cardinals.

4. B – July 13, 1982

5. C – 9

6. C – 2

7. A – True

8. D – 9

9. B – 2004

10. C – 2013

11. A – 4

12. B – False, Neither Bengie or José ever played for the Cardinals.

13. D – St. Louis Blues

14. A – Fundación 4 (Foundation 4)

15. B – 41

16. B – False, The St. Louis Cardinals drafted Molina.

17. C – 2

18. D – Ladislao Martinez High School

19. D – 0

20. A – True

# DID YOU KNOW?

1. Yadier Molina represented Team Puerto Rico in the 2006, 2009, 2013, and 2017 World Baseball Classics.

2. Yadier Molina holds the records for all-time games caught in the major leagues and the most postseason games played in the National League as of the end of the 2019 season.

3. In 2018, Yadier Molina was named to the MLB All-Star Team for the MLB Japan All-Star Series.

4. After Hurricane Maria ravaged Puerto Rico, Yadi and his wife Wanda set up a GoFundMe to raise $1 million in relief. The following season, Yadi was awarded the Roberto Clemente Award for his actions.

5. Yadier Molina was named to the All-World Baseball Classic Team twice.

6. Yadier Molina is the only catcher in Cardinals history to appear in at least five postseasons with the team.

7. In 2006, Yadier Molina became only the third player in MLB history to play in two World Series before the age of 25. The other two players? Johnny Bench and Yogi Berra. Pretty famous company on that record, Yadi.

8. After Tony La Russa's retirement, Mike Matheny took over as the Cardinals' manager. Mike Matheny was the Cards' starting catcher when Yadi made his MLB debut.

In 2001, Matheny told his wife, "I saw the kid that's going to steal my job." He became Yadi's manager 11 years later... Oh, and Yadi did totally steal his job.

9.  On Opening Day in 2010, Yadier Molina hit a grand slam. Only two other players in Cardinals history have done this—Mark McGwire and Scott Rolen.

10. On Opening Day 2020, Yadier Molina extended his Cardinals team record of Opening Day starts to 16.

# CONCLUSION

Learn anything new? Now you truly are the ultimate Cardinals fan. Not only did you learn about the Cardinals of the modern era, but you also expanded your knowledge back to the St. Louis Brown Stockings days.

You learned about the Cardinals' origins and their history. You learned about the history of their uniforms and jersey numbers. You identified some famous quotes and read some of the craziest nicknames of all time. You learned more about the famous Stan Musial, who is widely regarded as one of the best baseball players of all time. You learned more about the backflipping Ozzie "Wizard of Oz" Smith, as well as the powerhouse behind the plate, Yadier "Yadi" Molina. You were amazed by Cardinals stats and recalled some of the most famous Cardinals trades and drafts and draft picks of all time. You broke down your knowledge by outfielders, infielders, pitchers, and catchers. You looked back on the Cardinals' championships, playoff feats and the awards that came before, after, and during them. You also learned about the Cardinals' fiercest rivalry with the Chicago Cubs.

Every team in the MLB has a storied history, but the Cardinals have one of the most memorable of all. They have won an incredible 11 World Series championships with the backing of their devoted fans. Being the ultimate Cardinals fan takes a lot of knowledge and patience, which you tested with this book. Whether you knew every answer or were stumped by several questions, you learned some of the most interesting history that the game of baseball has to offer.

The history of the Cardinals represents what we all love about the game of baseball. The heart, the determination, the tough times, and the unexpected moments, plus the players that inspire us and encourage us to do our best because, even if you get knocked down, there is always another game and another day.

With players like Kolten Wong, Adam Wainwright, Yadier Molina, and Paul Goldschmidt, the future for the Cardinals continues to look bright. There is no doubt that this franchise will continue to be one of the most competitive teams in Major League Baseball year after year.

It's a new decade, which means there is a clean slate, ready to continue writing the history of the St. Louis Cardinals. The ultimate Cardinals fan cannot wait to see what's to come for their Redbirds.

Made in the USA
Coppell, TX
04 October 2022